eve

eve

CONTEMPORARY CUISINE

MÉTHODE TRADITIONNELLE

EVE ARONOFF

HURON RIVER PRESS

eve

CONTEMPORARY CUISINE

MÉTHODE TRADITIONNELLE

EVE ARONOFF

HURON RIVER PRESS

DEDICATION

This book is dedicated to my godfather, Larry Messé,
who loved food and wine as much as anybody could – and who was
always a source of knowledge, fun and inspiration to me.

Huron River Press
P.O. Box 7797
Ann Arbor, Michigan 48107-7797
www.huronriverpress.com

Food photography: Mark Thomas, Grand Rapids, Michigan
Photography assistant: Bob Hazen
Food stylist: Loretta Gorman
Location black and white photography: Chris Le Pottier
  with contribution from Greg Lewis
Book design: Savitski Design, Ann Arbor, Michigan

Printed and bound in Singapore

10 9 8 7 6 5 4 3 2

Library of Congress Cataloging-in-Publication Data

Aronoff, Eve, 1968-
  Eve : contemporary cuisine - methode traditionnelle / by Eve Aronoff.
    p. cm.
  Includes index.
  ISBN 1-932399-14-3
  1. Cookery. I. Title.
  TX714.A7565 2006
  641.5–dc22

                                        2006025207

TABLE OF CONTENTS

FOREWORD

How do new things come about? The brevity of the question belies its importance, especially to those of us in Ann Arbor with more than a passing interest in good food and eating. New dining possibilities enliven our explorations, discoveries, discussions, and, most important, opportunities to share these with friends who love great food.

A bit over three years ago eve became one of several new eating-places in town, immediately invigorating the food scene and food experience. The name itself sought to invoke, yet establish some distance from its guiding spirit: Eve the person, Eve the chef, indeed Eve, the personal chef. To little effect – Eve was there, at the restaurant, in the kitchen, in the food, in the décor, even, somewhat reluctantly, out among the customers, with thanks for their presence and plaudits. "Have you been to eve?" was soon the response to "Where can we go for dinner?" My daughter, who had become staunchly resistant to going anywhere for dinner, aspired to become a regular and began offering fervid commentary on everything from Roasted Pumpkin Soup, to each new pasta dish, Macadamia Encrusted Salmon and Pots-de-Crème. Oh, and apple crumble. She was not alone.

The restaurant's logo mantra – "Contemporary cuisine – méthode traditionnelle" – simultaneously captured and concealed the underlying, intensely "personal chef" commitment that Eve Aronoff brought to the venture from its beginnings – in the food, the décor, the music, the service, the wine, and both the kitchen and service staff. From my vantage point just around the corner from the kitchen door, eagerly observing the day-to-day developments, eve – The Restaurant seemed simply to be willed into existence, often against daunting circumstances. It arose from the wreckage of an earlier restaurant incarnation in the same space, not so much the conjunction of will and idea – too abstract – but of will and passion, a devotion that drew cheers and support from an often bewildering array of onlookers and hands-on helpers.

Eve's attention and care for each detail and preparation, from raw ingredients to the food served to each diner, injects the personal into eve – The Restaurant as well. As a supplier, I have enjoyed with gratitude eve – The Restaurant's zeal and enthusiasm in forging the link between what we bring to the restaurant, and what the restaurant's customers experience there. When Eve exclaims, "This is DELICIOUS!" you sense immediately that she is seeing people enjoy it, along with the personal touches that will accompany it.

For Eve/eve, "contemporary cuisine" means an imaginative drawing together of seasonings, ingredients and inspirations from West and North Africa, the Middle East and Southeast Asia, in personally intriguing combinations of new flavors and textures, pairings both complimentary and contrasting. And contemporaneous with what's freshly seasonal, local, vivid to the eye and palate – a theme that occurs in both the recipes and photographs in this book. Flavors that you see as you taste, contrasts that can startle with their seemingly effortless complementarity.

"Méthode traditionnelle" may evoke elements of classic French culinary technique from Le Cordon Bleu training, but it's more expansive than knife skills, stock and sauce making, sautéing, and plating. Tasting, experimenting, come into play – literally, play – a personal engagement with the food to be made and served, in anticipation of eaters' enjoying their own engagement. In other words, "method" equally familiar to Mario Batali, Thomas Keller, and to dedicated, imaginative home cooks.

Often, after enjoying an evening at eve – The Restaurant, and now looking over the recipes and photographs, I've felt that this joining of "contemporary" with "traditionnelle" leads to a food experience that I think my grandmother would cook for Sunday dinner if she had traveled around the Mediterranean basin and on to Southeast Asia, marketing and cooking as she went. And then returned to her own kitchen, to graft the experience on to her traditional southern-Midwestern culinary roots, to put something on the family table that was both new and yet distinctly her own. I think she would have immediately understood what Eve is about - and the kind of place that is eve – The Restaurant.

TR Durham

THANK YOU

I want to thank all of the people who specifically contributed to writing this book, but also to thank the people who helped to create and continue to support the restaurant – or else writing this book wouldn't have been possible. I thought I understood what I was getting into when I opened the restaurant – I had cooked for 14 years, worked my way up gradually, had been exposed to every aspect of a restaurant, was ready for the hard work, but when it opened I found out really quickly that I had no idea what I had gotten myself into. All day people were coming to me with questions I had no idea how to answer – I didn't really have a choice but to figure out how to answer them.

After three years with things at the restaurant going relatively smoothly (or as smoothly as they can go at a restaurant), I decided to write this cookbook. I found myself in the exact same situation – I had absolutely no idea what it really entailed or how consuming a project it would be – especially on top of the regular crazy schedule of running the restaurant. I always felt emotional when I read acknowledgements in other cookbooks because I could tell they were describing an intense experience, but I didn't really understand what they were going on and on about – Could it really be that hard?

But without the constant support of everybody involved with this book, and especially the restaurant staff, I really don't think that writing this book would have been practical to undertake. The countless hours of recipe testing, which because of the size of the kitchen, generally had to happen after dinner service, between midnight and the wee hours of the morning. The whole kitchen staff, especially Sergio Alcantara, Adan Garcia de la Cruz and Asa Schwartz who put in countless hours of recipe testing and are always willing to do whatever it takes. Armando Lopez, my original Sous chef / the most efficient person I know, who came back from his new job to spend his off days with us doing recipe testing (we know you will be back for good some day Armando!). Greg Lewis, our head waiter, who, as I started to stay at the restaurant later and later working on the cookbook, started to find projects he "had" to work on at the restaurant, keeping him there until all hours of the night until I realized he was just doing it for moral support and to keep me company. Erin Schumacher and Kara Vincent, who do all of the administrative work at the restaurant and give me peace of mind that things will be okay and go smoothly at the restaurant no matter what. The support from the staff at the restaurant is so steady that I could almost take it for granted, but even though writing this book has been incredibly consuming, I will always remember this time of writing the cookbook as the perfect moment in the life of the restaurant.

I want to thank Steve and Shira Klein, the publishers of Huron River Press, both for the opportunity to write this book and for putting up with me – as they have told me I am – hands down the most particular person they have ever worked with – but love me anyway – which, I think, is probably a pretty common perspective from the people I work with. I also need to thank Ron Reed, one of the partners in the restaurant for introducing us and encouraging me to write this book. I want to thank Mike Savitski, the graphic designer of the cookbook, for creating such a special book and truly capturing the feeling of the restaurant – Loretta Gorman, the food stylist, (and my partner at the photo shoots where we were always backing each other up to take just one more shot until we got it right – driving everyone else crazy) Mark Thomas and Bob Hazen, the food photographers, who somehow achieved our goal of taking the pictures with natural light in Michigan, in March which was a pretty challenging feat – Chris Le Pottier, my best friend since childhood, who used to put up photo collages in all of our friends' lockers in high school to surprise us and now whose gorgeous black and white photographs document every step of the restaurant – from demolition to build-out to now in the pages of this cookbook. Everybody involved has gone above and beyond the call of duty and made this book a real collaboration.

I want to thank all of the volunteer advisors and "editors" including my parents, Yaacov Rubin, Neal Robinson, Chris Le Pottier, Shana Kimball, Greg Lewis, Laurel Maguire and Tim Dugdale for their invaluable help. I especially want to thank my family and Yaacov Rubin for their ongoing support – it is a great feeling to know that there are people who will always be there for you if you need anything in or out of the restaurant. I am particularly grateful to Neal Robinson, one of the incredibly talented architect/designers of the restaurant from Wetsu, for being unbelievably generous with his time and ideas and acting as a design consultant throughout the process – Both Neal Robinson and Jason Young of Wetsu design for making the restaurant so beautiful that I had to try to live up to its aesthetics. I need to thank all of the partners in the restaurant, especially Dave Shipman and Peter Heydon, for supporting me through thick and thin – Judith and Reynold Lowe (and all of the other Ann Arborites) who, throughout the growing season, bring us beautiful and delicious ingredients from their farmhouse and gardens – from goose eggs, to arugula, to morels. I want to thank all of the farmers and purveyors whose ingredients inspire us and are captured in the photographs throughout the book – Renaissance Acres, Elegance Distributors, Gardenworks, Kurt Boyd's Croissant Shop, Monahan's Seafood Market, Morgan and York and especially our neighbor and great friend, TR Durham of Durham's Tracklements – Our customers who asked for so many recipes that I decided it would be just as easy to write this cookbook, as to keep sending out recipes via e-mail including all of the appropriate condiments and accompaniments included neatly in excel files (I was wrong). I would also especially like to thank Todd Wickstrom, who invited me to do a very special fundraising dinner at the restaurant to raise money for The Agrarian Adventure, a local project inspired by Alice Water's work building gardens in the schoolyards of San Francisco in her honor. Until that time, I had been immersed in expressing the values of the Slow Food Movement within the confines of the restaurant, but the invitation to be involved with The Agrarian Adventure dinner created new aspirations within me and opened up a new world for me – it opened my eyes to a bigger, broader way of cooking with a community of chefs and a world outside of the restaurant – And now, I feel I can capture and express those things that I care about within this book. Overall, I just feel very lucky to have had the opportunity to open the restaurant and to be able to write this book and I really hope you enjoy it.

Now, preparing for the book to go into its second printing I am thinking about the time that has passed and the people who have helped make the book a success and the restaurant strong. I want to express my appreciation to two people in particular, Sarah Normile and Ron Reed, whose steadfast, unconditional support, friendship and advice have helped me through all challenges and transitions and have helped to make the restaurant, day to day, a great place to spend my life.

Because I spend most of my time in the kitchen, people are usually surprised there is an Eve. Then, when they meet me, they always say that they pictured me a lot older – and then they say that they pictured me a lot more exotic – and with an accent. I am not sure how I developed my style of cooking, growing up in the Midwest for most of my life, but I have always been drawn to and loved to learn about far away places. I was a comparative literature major in college, and I think by reading books set in those distant cultures, I felt absorbed into and transported to those places. I especially loved reading about foods from warm and exotic cultures and those are the influences that have come together to define my style – West African, North African, Cuban, Vietnamese.

When I went to France, to study at Le Cordon Bleu, I learned the classical technique that allowed me to refine my cooking, but the food I make is still bolder in flavor and texture and pulls more from those age-old traditions than from the subtlety of classical French cuisine. A chef that I really admire once told me that there are basically two styles of cooking – one, focusing on a few, spare ingredients to really highlight them and the other, bringing together a variety of ingredients to combine into one complex taste. If that is true, then my style fits into the second. Evocative spices – curry leaves – dried limes – ingredients that are so aromatic they not only transform the taste of a dish, but bring up memories and images of places you've dreamed about going to, dreams and romantic ideals.

I love the combination of sweet, spicy and savory ingredients coming together with lots of textures and contrasts. Those textures and contrasts are an integral part of my style of cooking. While a dish may be spicy, complex or earthy, it is always best when paired with something pure, cool or bright to offset and bring out the best expression of both.

Those textures and contrasts carry through every aspect of the restaurant from the architecture and design to the smallest details like which flowers or what music we pick. The brick or grey wool or dark wood in the restaurant, cut by the simplest sheer gauzy white curtains, is the same as the minced Thai chicken in endive finished with a dollop of cool crème fraîche. To me, all of these elements echo and are inextricably tied to the food.

My approach to cooking may be traditional in following classical technique and in the commitment to making almost everything from scratch and to working with ingredients when they are in peak season, but is also modern in not following the restrictions of a single tradition or the conventions or rules of what is supposed to go together. Using your intuition – or your senses to bring you to what really goes together – being inventive, but never just for the point of it.

Some recipes in this book may seem somewhat daunting at first, but we wanted to allow you the option of making the dishes just as we do at the restaurant. Throughout the book we give suggestions on how to easily simplify and pare things down – you don't need to prepare every component and accompaniment included in a given recipe. We hope that you will find your favorites and improvise – mixing and matching them according to the season or your mood. We do the same thing at the restaurant throughout the year.

Many of the marinades, spice mixtures and aromatic oils are extremely versatile and keep well over time. Take an afternoon and make some of the spice mixtures to have on hand – they will keep well for several months stored in a cool dark place. Or, experiment with a few of the aromatic, infused oils or flavorful accompaniments like the Pickled Apples or Port Macerated Dried Fruit which will easily keep for several weeks. Stock your pantry with flavorful ingredients that keep well and go to the market a là minute for a few fresh ingredients and you will always be able to improvise and easily put together a great meal.

We tried to be specific in explaining the procedures and techniques that make a big difference in the results you achieve in your cooking. For example, choosing the right size pan so that the food you are sautéing will have enough room to sear and caramelize properly, instead of being crowded and essentially steaming in its own juices. When it comes to technique, it is important not to take shortcuts – it actually may only take a few seconds more to do something properly and that effort will definitely be worthwhile. The more you learn, from whatever source, the more knowledge you have to incorporate into your cooking repertoire and apply to whatever you may cook in the future.

While many of the recipes specify Michigan ingredients, local to us, it is always best to seek out what is special where you live. One of our favorite things to do is to discover special ingredients or foodstuffs from local farmers or small purveyors – not only are they likely to be the freshest ingredients – but it also adds a different level of excitement and personal involvement to the food you are preparing. For those items that we do not make from scratch, we have tried to be specific, pointing out favorite brands and makers that we've found – through a lot of trial and error – that really stand out.

Overall, we encourage you to be open-minded – leaving out a component or substituting ingredients doesn't matter as much as enjoying the experience of cooking and eating. We hope this book will be a source of sharing a mutual excitement about food.

DRINKS

AMANDA'S DREAM

ONE DRINK

This drink was created for one of our waitresses – Amanda – when she was reminiscing about her life in San Francisco and describing a delicious drink she used to love when she lived there. We have improvised a little bit, but she still says that drinking it always transports her back to San Francisco.

3 ounces Bailey's Irish Cream
½ ounce premium vodka
½ ounce Kahlúa
Splash of heavy cream
Brown Sugar Cream (see page 161)
Candied Orange Peel (recipe follows)

1   Combine first four ingredients with ice in cocktail shaker. Shake vigorously and strain into martini glass.

2   Top with Brown Sugar Cream and 2 pieces of Candied Orange Peel.

CANDIED ORANGE PEEL

1 orange, peeled avoiding white pith and cut into thin strips
1½ cups Simple Syrup (see page 24)
¼ cup sugar

1   Bring Simple Syrup to a simmer in small, non-reactive saucepan.

2   Add orange peel and simmer gently until candied, about 15 minutes.

3   Strain orange peel and combine in a small bowl with sugar tossing well – let sit overnight at room temperature – may be made several days in advance.

SANGRIA

8 GLASSES

This is a pretty unconventional, but very delicious sangria, and can be made throughout the year with almost any dried or fresh fruit that is in season.

2 cups dried apricots
1 cup globe grapes
½ cantaloupe, cut into large chunks
1 cup strawberries, stems removed and halved
1 apple, cut into large chunks
1 pear, cut into large chunks
½ cup chunks of lemons, limes and oranges
1½ bottles Ruby Port
1 bottle crisp Spanish or Chilean white wine (we use Veramonte or Basa Rueda)*
1½–2 tablespoons brandy
2 teaspoons freshly squeezed lemon juice
2 teaspoons freshly squeezed lime juice
¼ cup freshly squeezed orange juice
½ cup Simple Syrup (see page 24)
1 cup Looza passion fruit juice (or ¾ cup concentrated passion fruit drink)*
½ teaspoon cardamom seeds
1 teaspoon whole cloves

Combine all in a large non-reactive container, adjust to taste and let sit for at least eight hours and up to four days before serving.

Available at most Asian markets.

GINGER LIME MARTINI

ONE DRINK

1 ounce freshly squeezed lime juice
½ teaspoon fresh ginger, minced
1 tablespoon plus 1 teaspoon Simple Syrup
  (see page 24)
2 ounces premium vodka
1 tablespoon chopped crystallized ginger

1 Combine lime juice and fresh ginger and let sit
   for 1 hour.

2 Combine ginger and lime juice with Simple Syrup,
   vodka and ice in cocktail shaker. Shake vigorously
   and strain into martini glass.

3 Garnish with crystallized ginger.

JAMAICAN TENSPEED

ONE DRINK

1½ ounces Malibu coconut rum
1 ounce banana liqueur
1 ounce Midori
1 teaspoon heavy cream

1 Combine rum, liqueurs and cream.

2 Add ice and stir or shake lightly.
   Pour into medium Collins glass.

MOJITO

ONE DRINK

6–10 mint leaves
Splash of fresh lime
1½ teaspoons sugar
2–3 ounces premium white rum
Splash of 7-Up
Fresh sugar cane cut into thin stalk

1   Combine lime juice and sugar and use to macerate mint leaves.

2   Add rum and ice.

3   Finish with splash of 7-Up and garnish with sugar cane.

ESPRESSO MARTINI

ONE DRINK

1   demitasse freshly brewed espresso
1½ ounces premium vodka
1½ ounces Kahlúa
2   teaspoons Simple Syrup (see page 24)
½   teaspoon heavy cream (optional)

1   Combine first four ingredients with ice in cocktail shaker. Shake vigorously and strain into martini glass.

2   Add cream if desired.

TROPICAL FRUIT MIMOSAS

ONE DRINK

4   ounces favorite sparkling wine or champagne
2–3 ounces fresh tropical fruit juice such as guava, passion fruit, mango, or lychee
Drop rose water*

1   Combine ingredients.

2   Garnish with sliced, ripe tropical fruit such as star fruit, mangoes, kiwi, etc.

* Available at most Middle Eastern markets.

FRESHLY SQUEEZED LEMONADE

MAKES 2 GALLONS

2   cups hot water
3   cups sugar
3   cups ice
4   cups freshly squeezed lemon juice
2   cups cold water

1   Combine hot water and sugar and stir until sugar is dissolved.

2   Add ice and stir to bring to room temperature.

3   Add lemon juice and 2 cups cold water.

4   Taste and adjust by adding more lemon, sugar and water as needed.

YOUR GRANDMA'S ATTIC

ONE DRINK

*This is a drink that people either love or hate –
someone who really loved it once said it reminded
her of the smell of her grandmother's attic. Everyone
agreed and seemed to suddenly fall in love with it –
maybe in spite of that – or because of it – but that
is how it got its name.*

6 ounces sparkling wine
1½ ounces Disaronno Amaretto
1 brown sugar cube
1 orange wedge, for garnish

1   Place sugar cube and amaretto in a champagne flute.

2   Add sparkling wine and garnish with an orange
wedge or twist.

JAMTINI

ONE DRINK

*At the restaurant, we make these with my mom's
jams – everyone seems to have their personal
favorite that they request, which keeps my mom
busy making jam!*

3 ounces premium vodka
2 tablespoons Damson plum jam (see page 202)
   or other favorite jam

Combine premium vodka and jam in martini shaker.
Shake vigorously with ice and strain into martini glass.

POMEGRANATE MARTINI

ONE DRINK

¼ teaspoon Cointreau
¼ teaspoon Chambord
½ teaspoon pomegranate molasses*
2 teaspoons Simple Syrup (see recipe below)
3 ounces premium vodka
1 tablespoon pomegranate juice
1 wedge fresh pomegranate when in season, (generally between September and December)

Combine all ingredients with ice in cocktail shaker. Shake vigorously and strain into martini glass.

Available at most Middle Eastern markets.

WHITE GRAPE AND FRESH THYME MARTINI

ONE DRINK

2½ ounces Ciroc (French grape distilled vodka)
2½ ounces fresh or good quality white grape juice
2 teaspoons Simple Syrup (see recipe below)
2–3 broken sprigs fresh thyme
2 additional sprigs fresh thyme for garnish

1 Combine first four ingredients with ice in cocktail shaker. Shake vigorously to release the essence of thyme and strain into martini glass.

2 Garnish with fresh thyme sprigs.

SIMPLE SYRUP

MAKES ABOUT 1⅓ CUPS

1 cup sugar
1 cup water

Combine sugar and water in saucepan and bring to a boil, stirring until sugar crystals have dissolved. Cool to room temperature and store refrigerated in an airtight container.

When I went to France to go to culinary school, I thought I hated wine. I had grown up in a family where I was always encouraged to taste wine, as much as I was encouraged to eat or cook. I don't know if that was just the area I decided to rebel, but I decided I hated wine. The more I was around the French culture, the idea and presence of wine kind of seeped in and I developed an interest in, at least learning about, wine.

I decided to take the introductory level course in Wine and Spirits at Le Cordon Bleu. The first day of class, as I listened to our teacher describe the complexity of wine and the myriad of flavors it can consist of – from cherry to cedar to tar – I raised my hand and asked – "but, how do they get those flavors in there?" She looked really puzzled and like she didn't quite understand what I meant and asked me to repeat my question – she was fluent in English and so I couldn't understand why she didn't understand my question – why she kept asking me to repeat myself – so I tried to clarify my question and asked if the development of these flavors were in the form of extracts or syrups or concentrated reductions? When she finally realized that I sincerely wanted to know how the flavors of a wine get into the bottle, she was very kind and explained that development of these flavors are a naturally occurring part of the vinification process and while the flavors can be reminiscent of actual ingredients found in nature like cherries or lychees, the scents and flavors found in a wine actually come from the development of wild yeasts and a much more inexact, organic process. At the time, I didn't even know enough to know how silly my question sounded to everyone in the room. Anyway, I gradually ended up developing an insatiable appetite for learning about wine and as I learned about it my disdain for the taste of wine turned into a love/hate relationship and then finally falling head over heels in love with it. I went on to do pretty well in the class – to get my diploma in wine and spirits at Le Cordon Bleu and to start the process of working towards becoming a master of wine through the Wine and Spirit Education Trust in London. I am currently about 6 years into the program which is pretty intense and I don't know if I will ever finish – but I have learned that the more you learn about wine, the more you see there is to learn.

When I compare tasting wine with people here versus in France, it is a very different experience. Here, I find people immediately pronounce whether or not it is a good wine, definitively list the flavors found in the wine and make detailed analytical descriptions describing certain sensations across the mid–palate or forepalate. While in France, people tasting wine, no matter if they spent their whole life cultivating grapes and producing wine, just seemed to enjoy it, maybe closing their eyes and say something like…."good" or "mmm." All I know is that wine and wine and food pairing shouldn't be about feeling intimidated or about trying to prove yourself or how much you know. There are some indications of quality you can see or taste in a wine, clues that can help determine if it is a well-made wine – like the length of the finish – how long the flavor lingers in your mouth when you taste it – or how fine the bubbles are in a glass of champagne, but the majority of tasting and the appreciation of wine is subjective.

Our teacher once said that cedar to one person is somebody else's pencil shavings, and much of what you identify in a wine depends on your memories and what you have been exposed to in your life. Her advice to us was to pay attention to the scents around you – like roses or the smell of wet grass and remember those smells to call back when you taste a wine. Just like with cooking, I think the most important thing in tasting wine is to use your senses and to be open-minded in thinking about what flavors you pick out or what food it could pair well with.

Eye – includes determining what the wine looks like through the glass – if it is brilliant, limpid or cloudy. There are clues that can be found in examining the color of a wine. A white wine that has a greenish tinge can indicate youth, but if you open another bottle of the same wine over the course of the next several years, it will become more golden and finally orange or even brown as it continues in its evolution. A red wine might begin a purplish/black, then become red and then garnet and finally, when past its prime, brown. Different grapes have a tendency to produce different color juice and have a different weight or viscosity, which can be visible by looking at the wine. For example, the pinot noir grape tends to make wines that are jewel-like and translucent, or the Malbec or Tannat grapes, which yield a deep, almost black juice. These clues can give you an indication of what you are tasting and act as a head start for blind tasting. Look for the length of the "tears" or how long it takes the traces of the wine to slide down the side of your glass after you tilt the glass. Slow tears can be an indication of the level of alcohol in a wine as the process of the grape juice becoming wine is the result of the yeast converting the sugar in the grape must (juice) into alcohol – the tears can be an indication of the concentration of sugar in the must leading to a higher level of alcohol. **Nose** – when you smell the wine pay attention to both what you smell and how assertive or subtle those smells are. A high percentage of taste is actually made up of smell and what your nose is picking up. Smell is really important – **Swirl** the wine in your glass to aerate the wine and bring out even more expression of the nose. Smell it again – see how it has changed.

Mouth – taste the wine – pay attention to the flavors and the mouth feel – or weight of the wine in your mouth and how your mouth physically reacts to the wine. Acid causes your mouth to immediately salivate, while tannins, found in the skin and seeds of the grape can cause your mouth to dry or feel fuzzy. This reaction can help you determine whether you are tasting a very acidic or very tannic wine or a wine that has a nice balance between the two. Also pay attention to the actual weight of the wine in your mouth telling you if it is light, medium or full-bodied. Finally, the finish – this is how long the flavor of what you are tasting lingers and evolves in your mouth after you swallow it. The taste and how pleasing a wine is to you personally is subjective, but a long finish is generally a pretty good indicator of quality.

Paying attention to the taste of wine and food is the best bet for predicting a good marriage between the two. Just as with cooking, much of this is intuitive. Relax and think about what sounds good together. Pay attention to the flavors and interactions when you taste and then do it again the next time, incorporating what you have noticed. By doing this you will be developing your palate and your ability to make great food and wine pairings. The flavors of both wine and food change dramatically when you taste them together. You can't always predict this kind of interaction or what will make a great pairing, but there are some general guidelines that can help guide you towards making successful pairings. Instead of telling you a specific producer and vintage of a wine that you may not be able to get where you live to pair with the dishes in this book, I think it is more helpful to offer some of these guidelines to use as you learn and explore the art of food and wine pairing.

Progression of wines – Just as with tasting food, such as a series of cheeses, it is generally a good idea to start with the most delicate and subtle taste and build up to the most intense and complex. This is the ideal way to experience what each food or wine has to offer, without overwhelming your palate. As a general guideline, for the ideal progression of wines, begin with the lightest or most delicate and build in intensity of flavor, body and level of alcohol. For example, a four course meal could start with the Asian Smoked Salmon Tartare (page 38) paired with a crisp, bright white such as a Sancerre and progress to Curried Mussels (page 41) paired with a more expressive, aromatic white like an Alsace Gewurtzraminer or a German Kabinett level Riesling. The third course, Sweet and Spicy Moulard Duck Breast (page 103) could be paired with a New World Pinot Noir. For dessert, the Autumn Spiced Flan (page 168) could be paired with a decadently sweet, yet complex Sauternes – thus, returning to a white, but one that is sweet, complex and intense.

**Two approaches to pairing a wine with food –
To match or to contrast** – Either matching the weight and intensity of a dish or making a complimentary contrast can make successful pairings. For example, the Seared Scallops with Mango Cream (page 92) could go equally well with an electric German Riesling which would tie in with the fruitiness of the dish, but cut the creaminess – or a buttery, lightly oaked Napa Chardonnay to match the velvety, buttery scallops.

The more complex the wine, the more simple the food should be that you pair it with – The more complex a wine, the more important it is not to over-power it. If you want to really enjoy a wine with a lot of finesse, the simpler the food you pair with it, the better. For example, in order not to overpower the subtle nuances of a fine, well-aged Bordeaux, it is best to pair it with something as simple as roast lamb or beef. This is one of the primary reasons we always offer a "Simple Steak" on our menu at the restaurant. While our food is generally fairly highly seasoned and full of bold flavors and textures, we want our guests to have the option of really focusing on one of our cherished fine wines.

Think about the method of preparation – When selecting a wine to pair with a certain dish, keep in mind the cooking method used. For example, a piece of salmon is going to have a more intense flavor profile if it is grilled than if it is poached. Put that into consideration when thinking about the weight and intensity of the wine you are selecting.

Spicy, bold and exotic flavors – At the restaurant, our food is full of bold, intense and complex flavors. From Thai Minced Chicken in Endive (page 46), to Seafood with Curry Cream (page 97) to Braised Berkshire Pork Shoulder with Asian spices (page 106), we have paid a lot of attention and tasted a lot of wine to find great pairings for these potentially challenging dishes. While every dish may have its ideal match there are certain varietals and certain styles that lend themselves to these exotic flavor profiles. For whites – Alsace and especially Kabinett level German Rieslings and Gewürztraminers. Also, Brut and demi-sec Champagnes – and both dry and off dry New world Sparkling wines. For Reds – robust Red Zinfandels, spicy Shiraz or even a multi-faceted Pinot Noir. Some fortified wines also stand up really well and make great matches to intense flavors like salty foods paired with a Fino or Amontillado style sherry or a Bual style Madeira.

Fried Food – The best and easiest match for fried food is a wine with crisp acidity – for example, a crisp, clean, bright white wine such as an old or new world Sauvignon Blanc or a crisp, steely Chablis.

Cooking with wine and spirits – I love cooking with wine and spirits. Not just deglazing with a generic white wine, but incorporating interesting and high quality wines and spirits into the flavor profile of the dish you are making. Pairing these dishes with the same wine or spirit you have used in a recipe is a really interesting way to echo those flavors, and adds a different dimension or layer of flavor to the meal. You will see all kinds of wines and spirits throughout our recipes. For the Stir Fried Duck Salad (page 79) the Cured Duck, Apples, Pears and Roasted Sweet Potatoes are deglazed with a Muscat de Frontignan. The Inspired Lamb Pastry (page 110) incorporates golden raisins soaked in Pommeau du Normande, a unique Calvados seasoned with apple juice.

The Beef Tenderloin with Accoutrements (page 117) has, as one of its accompaniments, Macerated Dried Fruit (page 140) in which apricots, figs, dates and prunes are warmed gently in Ruby Port. Cooking with wines and spirits is just another way to extend your passion for them.

How to have a salad and still enjoy your wine – Vinegar is one of the most challenging ingredients to pair with wine – you basically don't want to do it. If you absolutely have to, you want to pair it with a wine with electric acidity like a super bright Kabinett level German Riesling. A better alternative is to replace the vinegar in a dressing with fresh lemon or lime juice or to dress your salad simply with good olive oil and a squeeze of fresh lemon or lime.

These are the butters we serve to begin each meal with our delicious bread baked by Avalon bakery in Detroit. These recipes make a generous amount, but they keep well and freeze well and are great to have on hand.

GUAVA

MAKES ONE ROLL

⅓ cup Guava Paste (see page 233) or use Goya Guava Paste in round tins*
¼ cup passion fruit syrup*
½ pound or 2 sticks unsalted butter at cool room temperature
½ pound or 2 sticks salted butter

1   Heat guava paste and passion fruit nectar stirring until smooth. Set aside and allow to come to room temperature.

2   Whip butter until fluffy and smooth.

3   Add guava paste mixture into butter and whip until combined.

4   Transfer to an airtight container or roll tightly into a log on a sheet of film wrap and then aluminum foil. Refrigerate or freeze for later use.

Available at most Asian markets.

FRESH HERB

MAKES ONE ROLL

1 pound or 4 sticks salted butter at cool room temperature
½ cup fresh chives, minced
¼ cup plus 1 tablespoon fresh basil, finely chopped
½ cup fresh mint, finely chopped
¼ cup fresh thyme, finely chopped
¼ cup fresh parsley, finely chopped
2½-3 tablespoons fresh garlic, minced
Kosher salt (optional)

1   Whip butter until fluffy and smooth.

2   Add herbs and garlic and whip until incorporated.

3   Taste and add salt if needed.

4   Transfer to an airtight container or roll tightly into a log on a sheet of film wrap and then aluminum foil. Refrigerate or freeze for later use.

SMOKED SALMON

MAKES ONE ROLL

1 pound or 4 sticks unsalted butter at cool room temperature
1 cup smoked salmon (ground)*

1   Whip butter until fluffy and smooth.

2   Add ground salmon and whip until incorporated.

3   Transfer to an airtight container or roll tightly into a log on a sheet of film wrap and then aluminum foil. Refrigerate or freeze for later use.

Available through Durham Tracklements, see sources, page 248.

FIRST COURSE

CUTTING BOARD
OF SMOKED AND CURED MEATS AND CHEESE

SERVES 4 – 6

This is one appetizer that I swore would always be on our menu. When I traveled through Europe there were so many small, neighborhood or country restaurants that always started you out with a simple cutting board of sliced, cured meats and cheese with simple, delicious accompaniments. It is such a convivial feeling to eat like this. This is our version and I think it makes you feel like you are sitting in a friend's living room or back in one of those neighborhood restaurants.

½ cup Basil Walnut Pesto (see page 231)
½ cup Marinated Olives (see page 133)
½ cup Fresh Herb Butter (see page 33)
½ cup Mustard Cream (see page 216)
Fresh herbs for garnish

1 ounce each of several types smoked and cured meat*
1 ounce each of several types artisanal cheese, cut into wedges**
Favorite crusty bread, we use cherry walnut – or French baguettes, sliced long and thin on the bias

1   Arrange sliced bread, cheese and meat in bundles on cutting board and garnish with fresh herbs.

2   Spoon Basil Walnut Pesto, Fresh Herb Butter, Mustard Cream and olives into ramekins and place on cutting board or platter.

*Available through Durham Tracklements, see sources, page 248.
**Available at Morgan and York or Zingerman's Deli, see sources, page 248.

ASIAN SMOKED SALMON TARTARE WITH PEPPERY GREENS AND LEMON SCENTED MAYONNAISE

SERVES 4

You can simplify this recipe by leaving out the Toasted Pumpernickel Rounds and peppery greens and instead spoon the Tartare into fresh endive leaves which will serve as as both a natural vessel for the salmon and a beautifully crisp garnish.

Asian Salmon Tartare (recipe follows)
¾ cup micro greens or baby arugula
1 teaspoon freshly squeezed lemon juice
Extra virgin olive oil
Kosher salt

Freshly ground black pepper
Lemon Scented Mayonnaise (recipe follows)
Toasted Pumpernickel Rounds (recipe follows)

1 Mix tartare gently just before serving to make sure vinaigrette is evenly incorporated.

2 Toss greens with lemon juice, a little bit of olive oil, a pinch of kosher salt and a few grinds of black pepper in a small non-reactive mixing bowl.

3 Spread each pumpernickel round lightly with Lemon Scented Mayonnaise.

4 Using a 2-inch biscuit cutter placed over pumpernickel round, place a heaping spoonful of tartare over toasted pumpernickel and press lightly into biscuit cutter.

5 Next, place a small amount of Lemon Scented Mayonnaise onto tartare and spread out with the back of a spoon to cover tartare. Gently remove biscuit cutter and top with a small bundle of dressed greens.

ASIAN SALMON TARTARE

2 cups smoked salmon – ground or cut into ⅛-inch dice*
2 tablespoons unseasoned rice wine vinegar (we use Marukan brand)**
¼ cup plus 2 tablespoons saké (we use Momokawa Pearl saké brand)**
1 tablespoon lemon grass, minced
1 tablespoon Gari (pickled ginger)**
1 tablespoon juice from pickled ginger
½ teaspoon sriracha, or more to taste (we use Shark brand)**
¼ cup light olive oil
½ teaspoon kosher salt or to taste

1 Heat rice vinegar and saké in a non-reactive saucepan, add lemon grass and pickled ginger to the warm saké mixture to infuse into the liquid.

2 Remove from heat and add pickled ginger juice and sriracha and allow to cool.

3 Drizzle in olive oil in a slow, steady stream while whisking to emulsify.

4 Pour vinaigrette over the ground salmon and mix gently by hand to incorporate. Add kosher salt and adjust seasonings to taste.

5 Let sit a minimum of 1 hour and up to 2 days – the texture and intensity will change over time, but will still be delicious.

*We use Tracklements Highland Smoked Salmon, see sources, page 248.
**Available at most Asian markets.

MAKES ABOUT 3 CUPS

You will have leftover remaining but is great to have on hand – keep refrigerated and use for up to 3 days.

3 egg yolks
2 tablespoons water
4 teaspoons fresh lemon juice
2 teaspoons Tabasco
1 tablespoon sriracha (we use Shark brand)*
¾ teaspoon kosher salt
1 cup light olive oil
½ cup extra virgin olive oil
½ cup finely sliced scallions
Zest of 1 lemon

1 Combine first 6 ingredients in food processor.

2 Drizzle in both oils in a slow, steady stream while food processor is running until thickened, but still light and supple.

3 Fold in scallions and lemon zest.

Available at most Asian markets.

TOASTED PUMPERNICKEL ROUNDS

½ loaf pumpernickel bread, sliced
Extra virgin olive oil
Kosher salt

1 Preheat oven to 375°F.

2 Cut pumpernickel into rounds using 2-inch biscuit cutters (or desired size) – bread will shrink slightly when baked.

3 Brush with extra virgin olive oil, sprinkle with kosher salt and lay out onto sheet tray.

4 Bake in oven until just crisp – about 5 minutes – remove from oven and let cool to room temperature.

SERVES 4 – 6

2 cups all-purpose flour
2 teaspoons sugar
2½ teaspoons baking powder
1 tablespoon kosher salt
2 eggs, mixed
½ cup buttermilk

1½ pounds conch, minced or pulsed into
    almost a paste in food processor
3 tablespoons pickled jalapeños, minced
¼ cup fresh chives, minced
¼ cup fresh cilantro, minced
¼ cup fresh parsley, minced

½ cup plus 2 tablespoons onion, minced
½ cup red bell pepper, minced
3 garlic cloves, minced
2 tablespoons capers, minced
3 tablespoons sriracha (we use Shark brand)

Light oil for frying

Sweet Chili Mayonnaise (see page 228)
Lemon Scented Mayonnaise (see page 228)
Cilantro Lime Salsa (see page 222)
Carrot Lime Purée (see page 226)
Crème Fraîche (see page 231)

1 Combine flour, sugar, baking powder, and kosher salt in a mixing bowl and set aside.

2 In a separate bowl combine eggs and buttermilk and set aside.

3 Combine the conch, pickled jalapenos, fresh herbs, onion, bell peppers, garlic, capers and sriracha in the bowl of a food processor and pulse ingredients until combined well.

4 In a large mixing bowl gently fold together the conch mixture with the dry ingredients until just combined, being careful not to over-mix or mixture will bind up and become tough. Add the liquid ingredients – folding together gently again being careful not to over-mix.

5 Heat oil in electric fryer or heavy pot to 350°F.

6 Fry a single spoonful of the conch mixture to determine if you need to adjust the seasoning – adjust seasoning as needed folding in gently and then continue frying dropping conch mixture by the spoonful into the hot oil – seasoning lightly with kosher salt immediately as you remove fritters from oil.

7 To serve – heap onto platter and accompany with any or all of the following – Sweet Chili Mayonnaise, Lemon Scented Mayonnaise, Cilantro Lime Salsa, Carrot Lime Purée, Crème Fraîche.

CURRIED MUSSELS

SERVES 4

1½ pounds mussels
3 tablespoons light olive oil
1 tablespoon fresh garlic, minced
1 tablespoon shallot, minced
Kosher salt
Freshly ground black pepper
4 fresh thyme sprigs
¼ cup dry, good quality white wine

1½ cups Curry Cream (see page 217)
1 tablespoon assorted fresh herbs, finely chopped, such as flat leaf parsley, chives, chervil, basil, thyme avoiding cilantro and rosemary as they may overpower the flavor of the other herbs
Crusty bread

1   Place fresh mussels in ice bath and stir. Discard mussels that do not close up tightly, drain well.

2   Sauté garlic, shallots, salt, pepper and a few sprigs of thyme in olive oil in large, shallow non-reactive pot.

3   Add mussels, shake to combine with garlic and shallots, add the white wine, thyme sprigs and season with kosher salt and black pepper.

4   Cover and steam for about 3 minutes.

5   Pour off half of liquid (discard or save for other use) and add Curry Cream.

6   Simmer covered until mussels are completely open – shaking the pan occasionally. Discard any mussels that do not open.

7   Adjust seasoning generously to taste.

8   Finish with chopped fresh herbs and serve with crusty bread for sopping.

SERVES 4

8 large, fresh, sea scallops, preferably dry scallops that have not been frozen, soaked or injected with saline
Moroccan Spice (see page 239)
Moroccan Seasoned Flour (see page 244)
2 tablespoons extra virgin olive oil
Kosher salt
Freshly ground black pepper

1½ cups Carrot Lime Purée (see page 226)
1 cup Crème Fraîche (see page 231)

1   Season scallops evenly and generously in the following order with kosher salt, lightly with freshly ground black pepper and moderately with Moroccan Spice.

2   Dredge in Moroccan Spice Flour, shake off excess and set aside.

3   Heat oil in large non-stick sauté pan and sear the scallops over high heat, making sure that they have enough space and are not crowded as this will cause the scallops to steam instead of being able to sear properly – move once to ensure that scallops don't stick to pan – lower heat to medium-high heat and continue cooking for about two minutes – turn the scallops and repeat process. Because the scallops are cooked so quickly, the extra virgin olive oil, which has a low smoke point, will actually help develop a deeper, richer color without burning.

4   To serve, spoon two concentric circles first of Carrot Lime Purée and second Crème Fraîche in center of each plate and then place scallops overlapping sauce.

SEARED SALMON IN RICE PAPER
WITH BASIL WALNUT PESTO

Every Thursday we offer complimentary appetizers in our wine bar – this is not only fun for our customers, but also gives the cooks in the kitchen a chance to experiment and put their passion for cooking to the test. I think every Wednesday night Aaron Lindell goes home thinking about nothing else but Thursday night "wine bar apps" and always comes back the next day with a couple of beautiful and delicious recipes – this is one of our favorites among Aaron's creations.

Six 2 x 2-inch squares salmon, 2–3 ounces each
6 sheets round rice paper (6 inch diameter is
　 desirable. If using 8 inch diameter, trim off
　 1 inch before making final fold.)
6 cilantro leaves (whole)

1 cup Basil Walnut Pesto (see page 231)
Kosher salt
Freshly ground black pepper
Light cooking oil
Sweet chili sauce (we use Mae Ploy brand)*

1　Season salmon lightly with salt and pepper.

2　Submerge rice paper in a bowl of warm water. After 3–4 minutes the rice paper should be soft and flexible – lay rice paper out on a flat surface.

3　Place one cilantro leaf in the center of the paper. Place one salmon over the cilantro, presentation side down.

4　Spread about 1 teaspoon of pesto over the salmon square (you will have some pesto remaining).

5　Neatly fold each side of the rice paper inward toward the center until you have a tightly sealed square. The rice paper should stick to itself. Continue this process until all the squares are wrapped.

6　In a lightly oiled non-stick pan over medium-high heat lightly sear (1 minute) each salmon square, pesto side down. This will seal the rice paper folds. Next, place in steamer basket over boiling water and steam each square for about 5-7 minutes depending on thickness. Wraps should be just firm to the touch when done.

7　To serve, drizzle plates or platter with sweet chile sauce and then arrange salmon packages on plate.

Available at most Asian markets.

1½ pounds chicken legs and thighs or
   half chicken, cut in pieces
2 cups Thai BBQ Marinade (see page 227)*
½ cup baby arugula chiffonade, (ribbon cut)
Kosher salt
Freshly ground black pepper
20 Belgian endive leaves, separated from
   one another

1 cup Crème Fraîche (see page 231)
2 cups Carrot Lime Purée (see page 226)

1   Preheat oven to 375°F.

2   Marinate chicken in half of Thai Peanut Marinade
    for 24 to 48 hours, tossing well to distribute
    marinade evenly.

3   Remove chicken from marinade and season
    generously with kosher salt and freshly ground
    black pepper.

4   Place in oven and roast until just cooked through.
    Internal temperature should rise above 150°F when
    checked with thermometer inserted into leg.

5   While chicken is roasting, place remaining marinade
    in a non-reactive saucepan and reduce on low
    heat until thickened. Remove from heat and let
    cool to room temperature. Stir to re-incorporate
    oil before use.

6   Remove chicken from oven and let cool to room
    temperature.

7   Separate chicken from bones and mince chicken.

8   Fold in chiffonade of baby arugula.

9   Season chicken generously to taste with reduced
    sauce, kosher salt and freshly ground black pepper
    (you may have some reduced sauce remaining).

10 Fill endive leaves with minced chicken and garnish
    with a small dollop of Crème Fraîche and Carrot
    Lime Purée.

WHOLE SPANISH OCTOPUS
DRESSED WITH SMOKEY TOMATO VINAIGRETTE

SERVES 4

We made this dish on the fly one night when a very special chef came to visit without a lot of advanced notice. Luckily, the restaurant is next door to an amazing fish market – Monahan's – and our Sous Chef Armando whipped up this vinaigrette based on a salsa he grew up with. This was the favorite part of the Chef's meal – it is slightly unusual, but simple and really delicious.

Whole Spanish octopus* (4 baby octopus about
   ½ pound each or 1 large octopus, about
   1½–2 pounds)
Kosher salt
Extra virgin olive oil
1½ cups Smokey Tomato Vinaigrette (see page 230)
Sliced warm baguette

Favorite olives such as Picholine, Nicoise or
   Arbequina or Marinated Olives (see page 133)

1   Place octopus into boiling salted water until just
   cooked through, about 30 to 40 minutes.

2   Toss in bowl with extra virgin olive oil and season
   to taste with kosher salt and freshly ground black
   pepper.

3   Dress with vinaigrette and accompany with additional
   vinaigrette, warm, sliced baguette and marinated olives.

*Available at Monahan's Seafood Market, see sources, page 248.

SERVES 4

3–4 cups heavy whipping cream
12 cloves garlic, peeled
1 Russet potato (½–¾ pounds)
1 pound smoked cod* (or use salt cod soaked
   overnight in milk and strained)
1–2 teaspoons fresh garlic, minced
1 tablespoon extra virgin olive oil
Kosher salt
Freshly ground black pepper

Puff pastry squares, split into top and bottom
   (see page 213 or purchase good quality,
   preferably from a pastry shop)
4 quail eggs
Light olive oil for frying

Spicy Greens, at warm room temperature
   (see page 140)

1   Bring cream and garlic cloves to a bare simmer
    in shallow saucepan and poach garlic for about
    20 minutes.

2   While garlic is poaching, cook potato by covering
    with cold water in a separate pot and bring to a boil.
    As soon as water boils add enough salt to be able to
    taste it in the water – continue cooking the potato
    until fork tender – remove potato from water, dry
    thoroughly, peel and discard skin and place in a
    mixing bowl covered with film wrap to keep warm.

3   After garlic has poached in cream for about 20
    minutes add smoked cod to garlic cream and
    poach for about 15 minutes – cream should start
    to thicken.

4   Lift cod out of garlic cream and add to mixing bowl
    with potato – strain garlic cream into measuring
    pitcher – adding poached garlic into bowl with
    cod and reserving strained garlic cream. You will
    have enough garlic cream for both seasoning the
    brandade and some remaining for final garnish.

5   Combine potato and cod, using a potato masher,
    and gradually incorporate extra virgin olive oil, garlic
    cream, minced garlic, kosher salt and freshly ground
    black pepper generously to taste, being careful not
    to over-mix or potatoes will bind up and become
    tight – Mixture should be very garlicky and flavorful
    and have the consistency of light, creamy mashed
    potatoes. Cover and reserve in a warm place.
    Reserve remaining garlic cream for final plating.

6   Fry quail eggs sunny side up in light olive oil and
    set aside.

7   To assemble, spoon brandade onto bottoms of
    puff pastry – top each with a small bundle of Spicy
    Greens and finally a sunny side up quail egg – spoon
    garlic cream over and around each and place puff
    pasty top alongside.

*Available through Durham's Tracklements, see sources,
page 248.

'CREAMSICLE'
SEARED SCALLOPS STUFFED WITH
MASCARPONE AND TANGERINES

SERVES 4

To simplify this recipe feel free to serve scallops atop the just-warmed mascarpone, instead of stuffing them individually

8 jumbo sea scallops, preferably dry scallops
   that have not been frozen, soaked or injected
   with saline, with incision ¾ way through center
Extra virgin olive oil
Kosher salt
Freshly ground black pepper
Juice of 1 orange or 3 tangerines

Zest of 2 oranges or 3 tangerines
1 cup mascarpone cheese
1 teaspoon confectioner's sugar
8 tangerine segments separated and skin and
   pith removed

Passion Fruit Beurre Blanc (see page 233)

1 Season scallops evenly with kosher salt and freshly ground black pepper.

2 Whip mascarpone with juice and zest of orange and carefully stuff scallops with mixture. You will have some mascarpone mixture remaining to re-stuff scallops if needed after cooking.

3 Heat oil in large non-stick sauté pan – begin to sear the scallops over high heat, making sure that they have enough space and are not crowded as this will cause the scallops to steam instead of being able to sear and caramelize properly – move once to ensure that scallops don't stick to pan – lower heat to medium-high heat and continue cooking for about two minutes – turn the scallops carefully, as to keep stuffing within scallop and repeat process. Because the scallops are cooked so quickly, the extra virgin olive oil, which has a low smoke point, will actually help develop a deeper, richer color without burning.

4 Remove scallops from pan. If some filling falls out – re-stuff gently and insert single tangerine segment into center of each scallop.

5 To serve, spoon Passion Fruit Beurre Blanc onto center of plate and place scallops over sauce.

SERVES 4

4 jumbo soft shell crabs, cleaned*
Kosher salt
Freshly ground black pepper
Curry Spice Mixture (see page 234)
Curry Spice Seasoned Flour Mixture (see page 244)
Light cooking oil

1 cup Fresh Mint Chutney (see page 218)
½ cup Crème Fraîche (see page 231)

1   Prepare crabs by seasoning generously in the
    following order with kosher salt, freshly ground
    black pepper and Curry Spice.

2   Dredge crabs in Curry Seasoned Flour and shake
    off excess.

3   Heat oil in non-stick pan and place crabs on
    their backs in hot pan – sear until golden, about
    2 minutes, turn over, and finish cooking, about
    3 more minutes.

4   To serve, make two concentric circles of first,
    Fresh Mint Chutney and second, Crème Fraîche
    in the center of each plate and lay crab just
    overlapping sauces.

*Fresh crabs should be alive just before cleaning or can
be cleaned for you by local fishmongers as close to
preparation time as possible. If cleaning crabs yourself,
place crab on its belly and 1) Cut off the front of the
face with kitchen shears and then press gently to extract
bile sac from opening, 2) lift flaps upward on each side
of crab and remove gills from underneath, 3) flip crab
over and remove apron from underside of body.

CHEESE CRAZY

I am obsessed with cheese. I was once a chef at a small, historic country club – we had only six entrees on the menu and the kitchen was so small that we didn't even have a walk-in cooler. But one day, the staff decided to count all of the cheeses we had in the kitchen to discover 28 different types!

At the restaurant, we incorporate so many interesting and delicious styles of cheese into our dishes – from appetizers to desserts. Aside from all of the cheeses incorporated into the recipes, we offer a cheese course before and after dinner and have a cheese cart on Thursday nights (that we don't really have space for in the dining room, but customers politely scooch out of the way, so we can maneuver around them).

The use of cheese is so widespread in our menu that we couldn't even figure out a way to have a chapter dedicated to cheese in this book. If we separated out all of the recipes that featured cheese, there would be almost nothing left in the main sections! Anyway, this picture is how I think cheese should be experienced – almost primal – encompassing everything from texture, to a suggestion of the possible tastes and smells, to the incredible history and traditions of artisanal cheese making.

INSPIRED NACHOS

The first restaurant I ever worked at made their nachos on wontons. I loved the texture of the crisp wonton chips, and that is the "inspiration" of the inspired nachos. It took us about six months after we opened to get people to start ordering these nachos. Nobody wanted to come to the restaurant to order something so mundane as nachos, but they are now consistently the favorite and most popular appetizer on the menu. Making these is a somewhat labor intensive project, but definitely worth it

Fried Wontons (recipe follows)
1 cup Slow Cooked Black Beans (see page 145)
½ cup Crème Fraîche (see page 231)

2 cups Cilantro Lime Salsa (recipe follows)
2 cups Cheese Mixture (recipe follows)
½ avocado, just ripe but still firm, sliced

1 Preheat oven to 375°F.

2 Place wontons on serving platter with Slow Cooked Black Beans in center. Cover generously with cheese mixture.

3 Place in oven until cheese is completely melted.

4 Top generously with Cilantro Lime Salsa, sliced avocado and dollop of Crème Fraîche.

CILANTRO LIME SALSA

3 ripe Roma tomatoes, medium dice
¼ cup scallions, sliced thin on a bias
¼ cup cilantro leaves, rough chop
½ teaspoon garlic, minced
½ teaspoon jalapeño peppers, minced and seeded
1¼ teaspoons fresh lime juice
½–1 teaspoon Chili Mélange (see page 242)
¾–1 teaspoon kosher salt
1 teaspoon extra virgin olive oil

Combine all and adjust seasoning.

FRIED WONTONS

10–12 wonton skins (we use Azumaya or Nasoya brand), cut into 3½ x 3-inch squares
Light cooking oil
Kosher salt

Deep fry wonton skins in 350°F oil. Season lightly with kosher salt immediately after frying and set aside at room temperature (may fry as early as 8 hours in advance and store at room temperature in air tight container).

CHEESE MIXTURE

Equal parts of the following:
Heaping ½ cup goat Gouda (we use Arena brand)*, shredded
Heaping ½ cup pepper jack, shredded
Heaping ½ cup sharp white cheddar, shredded

Combine all.

Available at Whole Foods Market, see sources, page 248.

ROASTED LOBSTER MUSHROOM
WITH SOFT SHELL CRAB, MAYTAG BLUE CHEESE
AND SCRAPED MICHIGAN CORN

SERVES 4 – 6

6 soft shell crabs, cleaned*
Kosher salt
Freshly ground black pepper
¼ cup Chili Mélange (see page 242) (You will need some for preparing soft shell crabs and some for seasoning crab mixture.)
1 cup Chili Mélange Seasoned Flour (see page 244)

¼ cup extra virgin olive oil
1 cup corn, scraped from the cob
4–6 lobster mushrooms, cleaned and split in half
¼ cup Maytag Blue cheese, crumbled
½ cup scallions, sliced on a long thin bias

2 cups Wild Mushroom Cream (see page 218)

1 Preheat oven to 400°F.

2 Prepare crabs by seasoning generously in the following order with kosher salt, freshly ground black pepper and spice mixture.

3 Dredge crabs in spice flour and shake off excess.

4 Heat oil in non-stick pan and place crab, on their backs, in hot pan. Sear until golden, turn over and finish cooking, about 3 more minutes. Cut into ½-inch dice and set aside.

5 Sauté corn quickly with extra virgin olive oil, seasoning with kosher salt and freshly ground black pepper – about 1 minute – and set aside.

6 Drizzle mushrooms with extra virgin olive oil and season with kosher salt and freshly ground black pepper. Roast about 10–12 minutes, remove from oven and set aside – then lower oven to 375°F.

7 In large mixing bowl gently toss together soft shell crab, corn, Maytag blue cheese, scallions, kosher salt, freshly ground black pepper and Chili Mélange to taste.

8 Spoon soft shell crab mixture onto mushroom and line up on sheet tray. Warm in oven for about 5 minutes or until hot and just golden.

9 To serve, spoon some Wild Mushroom Cream onto a plate and top with stuffed mushroom.

*Fresh crabs should be alive just before cleaning or can be cleaned for you by local fishmongers as close to preparation time as possible. If cleaning crabs yourself, place crab on its belly and 1) Cut off the front of the face with kitchen shears and then press gently to extract bile sac from opening, 2) lift flaps upward on each side of crab and remove gills from underneath, 3) flip crab over and remove apron from underside of body.

SMOKED COD CEVICHE

SERVES 4 – 6

This is another delicious dish created by Armando Lopez, my Original Sous Chef – and another dish highlighting TR Durham's of Durham's Tracklements absolutely incredible smoked fish.

1 pound smoked cod*(or salt cod soaked in water overnight and then strained)
¼ pound cilantro
¼ pound tomatoes, fine dice
2 tablespoons onions, fine dice
Kosher salt
Freshly ground black pepper

Light cooking oil
1 avocado, fine dice
½ – ¾ cup fresh lime juice
16 wonton skins, cut into squares, or other crunchy accompaniment such as tortillas, pita chips, or toasted baguette

1   Combine all ingredients except wontons gently in a non-reactive mixing bowl and set aside to allow flavors to meld together for 30 minutes.

2   Heat light cooking oil to 350ºF in deep fryer or deep saucepan. Fry wonton skins until golden – remove from oil onto paper towels and sprinkle immediately with a little kosher salt.

3   Spoon Ceviche over or alongside crisped wontons.

Available through Durham's Tracklements, see sources, page 248.

SERVES 4

TR Durham, of Durham's Tracklements contributed the recipe for these aromatic fresh sausages.

1 pound ground pork
2 tablespoons fish sauce
1½ teaspoons brown sugar
⅓ cup shallots, minced
3 garlic cloves, minced
1 small stalk lemon grass, minced
¼ cup coriander stems, minced
1 teaspoon ginger, minced
1 tablespoon shredded unsweetened coconut

Kosher salt
Freshly ground black pepper
Light cooking oil

1 cup Maple Cream (see page 163)
1 cup Exotic Fruit Chutney (see page 219)
Fresh mint leaves

1   Combine first 9 ingredients gently in bowl being careful not to overwork or meat will bind up and become tight.

2   Form a single teaspoon of mixture into a patty, season lightly with kosher salt and freshly ground black pepper, and cook in a small sauté pan with a little oil. Taste to determine whether the rest of the batch needs additional seasoning – adjust seasoning as needed, incorporating gently as to not overwork meat.

3   Divide sausage mixture into 8 patties – first forming gently into balls and then flatten gently as to not overwork mixture.

4   Season patties with kosher salt and freshly ground pepper. Heat oil in large sauté pan and sauté until just cooked through – about 2–3 minutes per side.

5   Pour off excess oil and deglaze pan with Maple Cream simmering until cream thickens and small bubbles form – about 1 minute.

6   Serve sausage over Maple Cream and accompany with Exotic Fruit Chutney and fresh mint leaves.

SOUPS AND SALADS

PURÉE OF CURRIED ROAST PUMPKIN, SWEET POTATOES AND APPLES

SERVES 6 – 8

Extra virgin olive oil
Salted butter
1 large Spanish onion, fine julienne (about 2 cups)
Kosher salt
Freshly ground black pepper
1 large pie pumpkin, cut into wedges (about 2 pounds)
1–1½ teaspoons, or to taste hot curry powder* – good quality or mix yourself (see page 234)
2 large sweet potatoes, cut into large cubes
2 large Granny Smith apples, sliced
3 cups Chicken Essence (see page 68) stock or broth (If using canned broth, use College Inn brand.)

2 cups half and half
¾ cup Brown Sugar Spice (see page 242)
2 tablespoons Curry Spice Variation One (see page 238) or your favorite curry powder
1 tablespoon plus 1 teaspoon sriracha (we use Shark brand)**

Rum Macerated Golden Raisins (recipe follows)

1 Combine curry spices and set aside.

2 Preheat oven to 475ºF.

3 Sauté onions in olive oil in large non-reactive saucepan until very soft – season with kosher salt and pepper.

4 Sprinkle pumpkin wedges generously with olive oil, kosher salt and pepper and roast in oven until soft and starting to brown and blister. Remove from oven and scoop flesh from skin.

5 Roast sweet potatoes as you did the pumpkin above.

6 Sauté apples with small amount of olive oil and butter in large sauté pan – season with 1 teaspoon of the Curry Spice.

7 Purée pumpkins, sweet potatoes, apples, and onions in batches in food processor.

8 Combine purées in large, non-reactive stock pot. Add chicken stock or broth, Brown Sugar Spice, sriracha, Curry Spice and kosher salt and freshly ground black pepper (to taste) and bring to a simmer.

9 Add half and half and continue to simmer until purée thickens slightly.

10 Adjust seasonings generously to taste.

11 Garnish with zest of oranges and chopped golden raisins tossed with dark rum.

RUM MACERATED GOLDEN RAISINS

½ cup golden raisins, rough chopped
2 tablespoons dark rum
Zest of one orange

Toss the zest of oranges and raisins in the dark rum and let rest for at least 30 minutes.

*Available through Penzey's Spices, see sources, page 248.
**Available at most Asian markets.*

JEWISH CHICKEN SOUP
WITH OR WITHOUT MATZOH BALLS

SERVES 4

This chicken soup is, again, not very traditional, but many people have said that it is the best chicken soup they've had in their lives. Sometimes we spend up to an hour just seasoning this soup – adding a drop more sriracha, a few more grinds of black pepper, a little more kosher salt to get it just right (but that's also an excuse to keep tasting it). The matzoh balls are delicious also – the perfect balance between "sinkers" and "floaters."

1 whole chicken, about 3 pounds, cut into 6–8 pieces
2½ quarts Chicken Essence (see page 68), stock
   or broth (If using canned broth, use College
   Inn brand.)
2 carrots, cut at a bias
3 stalks celery, cut at a bias
1 onion, fine julienne
3 leeks, fine julienne
3 cloves garlic
2 cups corn, scrape from the cob or frozen kernels

1½ cups packed fresh basil, leaves torn
½ teaspoon crushed red pepper flakes
1 tablespoon sriracha (we use Shark brand)*
1–1½ teaspoons hot sauce (we use Melinda's brand)
¼ teaspoon crushed red pepper
¼ teaspoon freshly ground black pepper
2 teaspoons kosher salt, or more to taste
Matzoh Balls (recipe follows) or ½ pound Rusticella
   Fusilli or other good quality pasta, cooked al dente
   either in salted boiling water or salted boiling
   stock/broth

1 In large pot bring Chicken Essence or broth to
   gentle simmer. Add chicken pieces and cook for
   about 30 minutes.

2 Remove chicken and add remaining ingredients with
   the exception of corn, basil and Matzoh Balls.
   Continue to simmer for about 20 minutes.

3 Meanwhile, separate chicken meat from bones
   and skin and then add back into pot.

4 Remove from stove and add torn basil leaves and
   corn – adjust seasonings generously to taste –
   should be very flavorful.

5 Finish with Matzoh Balls or pasta.

Available at most Asian markets.

MATZOH BALLS

4 eggs
¼ cup Schmaltz (rendered chicken fat)
   or melted butter
1 cup matzoh meal
½ cup Club Soda
1 teaspoon plus a pinch of kosher salt
Pinch of pepper

1 Beat eggs.

2 Add remaining ingredients and mix gently
   just to combine.

3 Store and refrigerate for at least 2 hours.

4 Fill medium stockpot halfway with cold water and
   2 teaspoons kosher salt and bring to a boil.

5 Wet hands and form mixture into balls about
   2-inches in diameter.

6 Place matzoh balls in boiling water and reduce
   to a simmer and cover. Cook for 15 minutes.

7 Remove and put into warm chicken soup to hold
   until needed.

AROMATIC LENTIL SOUP

SERVES 6

This recipe evolved from one of my favorite cookbooks, Fields of Greens *cookbook from the very special* Greens *restaurant in San Francisco.*

1 cup lentils
4½ cups water
Kosher salt
1 tablespoon extra virgin olive oil
½ medium yellow onion, fine dice
1½ teaspoons Kosher salt
½ teaspoon cayenne pepper
½ small carrot, fine dice
½ celery rib, fine dice
½ small red or yellow bell peppers, fine dice
1½ teaspoon cumin seeds, toasted and ground
1 teaspoon ground coriander
¼ teaspoon ground turmeric

1 tablespoon garlic, minced
2 tablespoons fresh ginger, grated
1½ cups canned tomatoes with juice, medium dice
½ cup cilantro, minced
¼ jalapeño, seeded and minced
1 teaspoon red wine vinegar
1 heaping teaspoon sugar
½ heaping cup grated Parmigiano Reggiano or aged provolone

½ cup fresh mint chiffonade, (ribbon cut)
1 cup Crème Fraîche (see page 231)

1 Sort and rinse lentils and place them in a soup pot with the cold salted water. Bring to a boil, reduce to a simmer, uncovered, until tender, about 20 minutes.

2 While lentils are cooking, heat the olive oil in sauté pan and add the onions, salt and cayenne. Cook over medium heat until the onions are soft, and then add the vegetables and the spices.

3 Stir in garlic and ginger and cook for a few more minutes.

4 Add the vegetables and tomatoes to the lentils and their broth. Cover and simmer gently until soup has thickened and flavor has deepened.

5 Adjust seasonings to taste. Add vinegar, sugar and Parmigiano Reggiano – stir to combine and remove from heat. You may pulse with hand emulsifier wand to obtain smoother consistency.

6 Adjust seasoning generously and garnish with Crème Fraîche and mint chiffonade.

BLACK BEAN CREAM

SERVES 4

7 garlic cloves, whole
½ medium onion, rough chop
¼ yellow bell pepper, rough chop
¼ green bell pepper, rough chop
¼ red bell pepper, rough chop
½ jalapeño or other chili pepper, rough chop
¾ cup bacon, medium dice
2 Roma tomatoes, medium dice
4 cups cooked black beans (or if using canned, use El Ebro brand)*
1 tablespoon sriracha (we use Shark brand)**
2 bay leaves
¼ teaspoon or a couple of drops red wine vinegar
2 heaping tablespoons canned puréed chipotle peppers in adobo (puréed with sauce)

1–2 teaspoons kosher salt
Pinch of freshly ground black pepper
1 teaspoon ground cumin
1 teaspoon dried oregano
Pinch of sugar, or to taste
2 cups, or to taste Crème Fraîche (see page 231)
1 cup, or to taste Chicken Essence (see page 68) stock or broth. (If using canned broth, use College Inn brand.)
¼ cup additional chipotles
Kosher salt
Freshly ground black pepper

Crème Fraîche (see page 231)
Cilantro Lime Salsa (see page 222)

1 In food processor, purée garlic, onions, bell pepper and jalapeños.

2 In a wide, shallow braising pan, render bacon over medium heat. Remove remaining pieces of bacon leaving fat in pan.

3 Place ingredients from food processor into pan with hot bacon fat and sauté, stirring frequently until liquid has evaporated.

4 Add tomatoes and sauté 5 minutes.

5 Add beans, chipotle peppers, sriracha, bay leaves, cumin, oregano, kosher salt and freshly ground black pepper. Simmer until thickened.

6 Add red wine vinegar and sugar to taste.

7 Stir in Crème Fraîche and Chicken Essence/ stock/broth.

8 Season to taste with additional puréed chipotles, kosher salt and freshly ground black pepper. Remove bay leaves before serving.

9 Serve garnished with Crème Fraîche and Cilantro Lime Salsa.

*Available at most Latino markets.
**Available at most Asian markets.

ESCARGOT CREAM

SERVES 4 – 6

1½ pounds mussels
1 tablespoon garlic, minced
1 tablespoon shallots, minced
¼ cup Pernod plus a splash to finish
¼ cup Amontillado sherry
2½ cups cream
2½ cups half and half
10 garlic cloves

Two 8 ounce cans, escargot, rinsed gently under
    cool water for about 5 minutes
½ teaspoon lobster base or Thai dried shrimp paste*
1 tablespoon tarragon, minced
¼ cup speck or hard salami, minced

1 small black truffle, optional
Crème Fraîche (see page 231)
Reggianno Tuiles (recipe follows)

1 Place fresh mussels in ice bath – swirl mussels
   around in ice and discard mussels that do not
   close up – drain well.

2 Sauté garlic, shallots, in olive oil in a large, wide
   non-reactive pot, and season with salt and pepper.

3 Add mussels, stir, sauté for a few minutes and
   add both Pernod and sherry to deglaze; cover pot
   shaking often until mussels open (about 5 minutes).
   Remove from heat when most mussels open.

4 When cool enough to handle remove mussels from
   shells and set aside, discarding shells and reserving
   remaining broth.

5 Meanwhile, in medium stock pot or large saucepan
   poach garlic cloves in cream and half and half for
   20 minutes at a bare simmer – add escargot and
   poach for an additional 20 minutes.

6 In food processor or with hand emulsion blender
   purée escargot, garlic, cream and mussel broth.
   Incorporate lobster base or shrimp paste.

7 Return to stove, bring to a gentle simmer and stir
   in tarragon, speck or salami and an additional splash
   of Pernod – adjust seasonings generously to taste.

8 Garnish with Crème Fraîche and Reggiano Tuiles.

REGGIANO TUILES

1½ cups Parmigiano Reggiano, shredded

1 Heat oven to 300°F.

2 Line sheet tray with a silpad (available at most
   cooking shops).

3 On sheet tray divide shredded Reggiano into 6 even
   piles, flatten gently into circles and place in oven to
   bake until golden.

4 Remove from oven and let cool to room temperature
   before removing from sheet tray.

Available at most Asian markets.

CHICKEN ESSENCE

This is a concentrated chicken stock that honestly takes a ridiculous amount of bones to yield a very small amount of essence – but it is incredibly rich and flavorful and can really make your soup special. If you don't reduce it all the way down it will be a delicious stock – if you continue to reduce it that is when it becomes an essence.

14 pounds chicken backs, necks, thighs, wings
6 quarts water
3 large onions, quartered
2 leeks, white and light green parts julienned*
2 parsnips
2 cups celery leaves, chopped
8 sprigs fresh parsley

6 garlic cloves, whole
2 large shallots
4 medium carrots, cut into 4-inch lengths
2 cloves
1½–2 tablespoons kosher salt
8 whole peppercorns

1 Wash chicken pieces and place in stockpot. (If you do not have a pot large enough, divide ingredients evenly between two large stock pots and proceed with instructions) Cover with water and bring just to a boil. Reduce to a simmer and skim surface with large flat spoon or ladle to remove impurities.

2 Add remaining ingredients and simmer with cover slightly ajar so it is not tightly closed. Skim impurities from surface as needed for about 3 hours.

3 Lift chicken and bones from stock and strain through fine sieve or colander lined with double layer of cheesecloth, pressing with back of ladle to extract as much flavor as possible.

4 Return to pot and reduce at gentle simmer until liquid reduced by half, to about 2½ quarts.

*Leeks can be very sandy and somewhat difficult to clean as the grit is often hidden between the leeks many layers. I have found the best method of cleaning leeks is to cut leeks in half widthwise and then in half lengthwise. Then, place in large bowl of cold water – swishing around to loosen and remove grit – lift leeks out of water (don't pour sandy water over leeks). Discard dirty water and refill bowl with clean cold water – repeating process a few times, as necessary.

WILD MUSHROOM CREAM

SERVES 4

We make this soup throughout the year with different mushrooms as they come into their prime season. It is amazing to see how the flavor changes from using chanterelles to cèpes to hedgehogs, etc. It is also absolutely delicious, however, with any combination of mushrooms readily available at the market – shiitakes, portabellas, crimini and button.

1½ tablespoons fresh shallots, minced
1½ tablespoons fresh garlic, minced
1½ pounds assorted, wild, cultivated mushrooms, sliced or torn into equivalent sized pieces
1-2 teaspoons kosher salt
Freshly ground black pepper
⅔ cup sherry (we use Lustau Amontillado Sherry)
3 cups Chicken Essence (see page 68) stock or broth (If using canned chicken broth, use College Inn brand.)

2 cups heavy whipping cream
2 cups sour cream
1 cup Parmigiano Reggiano or aged provolone, grated, (we use ½ cup each)
¾ cup fresh herbs, chopped, such as flat leaf parsley, chives, chervil, basil, thyme avoiding cilantro and rosemary as they may overpower flavor of other herbs

Crème Fraîche (see page 231), for garnish

1   Sweat shallots and garlic with some kosher salt on medium-low heat.

2   Add mushrooms and raise heat to medium-high until mushrooms exude liquid. Simmer until liquid is almost completely gone. Season generously with kosher salt and freshly ground black pepper.

3   Deglaze with sherry and cook for a few minutes, or until sherry is incorporated with mushrooms.

4   Add chicken stock and cream and reduce until mixture thickens and coats the back of a spoon.

5   Temper with sour cream by adding some of the sauce to the sour cream and then adding sour cream back into the sauce.

6   Simmer until slightly thickened.

7   Add cheese and ½ cup of fresh herbs, adjust seasonings and then immediately remove from heat.

8   Garnish each bowl with a dollop of Crème Fraîche and additional chopped herbs.

*This soup was invented serendipitously one day when we had made too much gratin and not enough soup!
If you have leftover gratin it is the easiest soup in the world to make, because it starts out with so much flavor.
Even if you are starting from scratch by making the gratin I think it is worth it for the result you get. It is
surprisingly versatile – we have accompanied it with everything from thick-cut bacon, to snipped chives
to Sea Urchin roe and even people who don't like sweet potatoes go crazy over it.*

1 pan Gingered Sweet Potato Gratin (see page 151)
3 shallots, minced
2 tablespoons olive oil
3 tablespoons good quality dry white wine
3 cups heavy whipping cream
3 cups Chicken Essence(see page 68), stock or broth
   (If using canned broth, use College Inn brand.)
2 teaspoons lobster base or Thai dried shrimp
   paste*, or to taste

½ teaspoon ground coriander
¼ teaspoon cayenne, or to taste
2 teaspoons kosher salt, or to taste
Freshly ground black pepper to taste

1 cup Crème Fraîche (see page 231)
Fresh chives, snipped

1 Sweat shallots in olive oil with kosher salt and
   freshly ground black pepper.

2 Deglaze with dry white wine.

3 Add cream and stock (or broth) gradually and bring
   just to boil – then reduce to a simmer.

4 Add gratin and lobster base (or shrimp paste) and
   either purée with hand emulsifier or transfer to
   food processor to purée.

5 Return to stove and bring to a gentle simmer until
   sauce has thickened slightly. Season with cayenne
   and additional kosher salt and freshly ground black
   pepper as needed.

6 Garnish with Crème Fraîche and fresh snipped chives.

Available at most Asian markets.

GAZPACHO

SERVES 4

6 Roma tomatoes
5 cucumbers
1 medium red onion
1 red bell pepper
1 yellow bell pepper

1 heaping tablespoon fresh minced garlic
14 ounce can whole tomatoes
2 tablespoons red wine vinegar
½ cup extra virgin olive oil
1 tablespoon Kosher salt
1 teaspoon freshly ground black pepper

2 teaspoons hot sauce (we use Melinda's brand)
¼ cup freshly squeezed lime juice
1 teaspoon hot pepper paste (we use Amores
  brand Italian hot pepper paste)
1–2 tablespoons canned chipotle in adobo, puréed
¼ cup assorted chopped fresh herbs such as chives,
  tarragon, basil, sage, mint, flat leaf parsley, avoiding rosemary and cilantro as they may overpower
  flavor of other herbs

Crème Fraîche (see page 231)
Garlic and Herb Croutons (see page 72)
Additional fresh torn basil to garnish

1   Cut half of tomatoes, cucumbers, red onion and bell
    peppers into medium dice and reserve the rest.

2   Purée the remaining half of tomatoes, cucumbers,
    red onion and bell peppers in food processor.

3   Combine vegetables, both chopped and puréed,
    with remaining ingredients in large, non-reactive
    bowl and adjust seasonings generously to taste.

4   Garnish with Crème Fraîche, Garlic and Herb
    Croutons and fresh torn basil.

6 cups assorted mixed greens, shoots and flowers
(We use mâche, frisée and arugula greens and
buckwheat, sunflower and pea shoots and
whatever else looks best at the market.)
Heaping ¼ cup basil chiffonade, (ribbon cut)
Heaping ¼ cup mint chiffonade, (ribbon cut)
Kosher salt
Freshly ground black pepper
Vinaigrette or dressing of your choice
(see pages 229–230)

1 In large mixing bowl, gently toss greens and herbs
with vinaigrette and a pinch of kosher salt and
freshly ground black pepper.

2 Place greens onto each plate and accompany with
Garlic Herb Crouton and small wedge of cheese.

4 Garlic and Herb Croutons (recipe follows)
Four ½ ounce wedges of favorite artisanal cheese
to adorn crouton (We vary ours throughout
the year.)

GARLIC AND HERB CROUTON

MAKES ABOUT 6 CROUTONS

½ cup extra virgin olive oil
¼ cup light oil
½ cup garlic, minced
½ cup mixed herbs such as flat leaf parsley, chives,
chervil, basil, thyme avoiding cilantro and rosemary as they may overpower flavor of other
herbs
Kosher salt
Baguette, sliced on a bias as long and thin
as possible

1 Preheat oven to 275°F.

2 In saucepan heat oil, and then add garlic, stirring
until garlic puffs up becoming white and fragrant.

3 Let cool to room temperature and add herbs.

4 Lift garlic herb mixture out of oil with a slotted
spoon and smooth an even layer onto sliced bread
pressing lightly into bread. Sprinkle lightly with
kosher salt. Turn over and repeat.

5 Place sliced bread on baking sheet lined with parchment paper and bake until just golden. Bread should
dry out and become crisp and garlic should begin to
just turn golden but not brown.

WINTER SALAD OF SHAVED FENNEL WITH BLOOD ORANGES, PINK GRAPEFRUIT, AND POMEGRANATE

SERVES 4

1 fennel bulb, sliced as thin as possible
½ red onion, fine julienne
½ cup blood orange segments, all membrane and pith removed
½ cup pink grapefruit segments, all membrane and pith removed
½ cup kumquat, sliced thin
½ cup pomegranate seeds

¾ cup Guava Citrus Vinaigrette (see page 229)
1 watermelon radish, sliced into thin rounds*
1 head radicchio, leaves separated

1 cup Exotic Fruit Chutney (see page 219)

1 In non-reactive stainless-steel bowl combine first seven ingredients and toss.

2 Assemble salad by placing radicchio leaf with single slice of watermelon radish tucked inside.

3 Fill with salad mixture and accompany with Exotic Fruit Chutney.

*Available at Gardenworks farm stand at Ann Arbor Farmer's Market.

BLACKENED FLANK STEAK

SERVES 4

½ cup Chili Mélange (see page 242)
Kosher salt
Freshly ground black pepper
Four 4–6 ounce portions flank or skirt steak
6 cups mixed greens (We use mâche, frisée and arugula greens and buckwheat, sunflower and pea shoots and whatever else looks best at the market.)

1 cup Fricassee of Wild Mushrooms (see page 136)
12 pear or grape tomatoes
½ red onion, fine julienne
¾ cup Maytag blue cheese, crumbled
¾ cup Balsamic Vinaigrette (see page 229)

1 Blacken steak by cooking in a piping hot cast iron skillet about 3 minutes per side until medium rare or desired level of doneness.

2 Let rest about 5–7 minutes in lightly tented foil and then slice against the grain at a wide angle as thinly as possible.

3 Make salad by gently tossing greens with vinaigrette and a pinch of kosher salt and freshly ground black pepper – you may have some vinaigrette left over.

4 Arrange greens on plates and top with bundle of warm Fricassee of Wild Mushrooms. Sprinkle with tomatoes, red onion and Maytag blue cheese and finally, fan out sliced blackened flank steak.

SERVES 4

6 cups assorted mixed greens (We use mâche, frisée, arugula and buckwheat, sunflower and pea shoots and whatever else looks best at the market.)

3 cups assorted seasonal vegetables (varies throughout the year but some of our favorites are julienned red onion, red, yellow and orange bell peppers, sugar snap peas, heirloom tomatoes, radishes, roasted beets, avocado and ramps)

Light olive oil

Four 6-ounce pieces wild king salmon (see page 74), or farmed-raised salmon when wild is not in season
Kosher salt
Freshly ground black pepper
Chili Mélange (see page 242)
Chili Mélange Seasoned Flour (see page 244)

1½ cups Balsamic Vinaigrette (see page 229)
½ cup shredded or shaved Parmigiano Reggiano
Freshly squeezed lime juice

1 Preheat oven to 400°F.

2 Prepare greens and vegetables and keep in a cool place until ready to toss salad.

3 Heat oil in non-stick pan.

4 While oil is heating, prepare fish by seasoning generously in the following order with kosher salt, freshly ground black pepper and Chili Mélange.

5 Dredge fish in Seasoned Flour and shake off excess.

6 Place fish, presentation side down, in hot pan – sear until golden, turn over, and place in oven until fish is just cooked – should take about 10 minutes per inch thickness of fish.

7 While fish is cooking, dress greens with Balsamic Vinaigrette and toss gently.

8 Sprinkle salad with Regianno and place bundles of vegetables around the perimeter of salad.

9 Remove salmon from oven and dress with a squeeze of fresh lime – place in center of each salad and serve.

MOZZARELLA DI BUFFULA
WITH SMOKEY TOMATO VINAIGRETTE AND PROSCIUTTO CROUTONS

SERVES 4

1 pound fresh mozzarella di Buffula, sliced into 12 slices
½ pound prosciutto, ½-inch thick slice
½ red onion, fine julienne
1 large or 2 medium heirloom tomatoes
6 cups mixed greens, (We use mâche, frisée and arugula greens and buckwheat, sunflower and pea shoots and whatever else looks best at the market.)

1 cup Smokey Tomato Vinaigrette (see page 230)
Kosher salt
Freshly ground black pepper

1 Preheat oven to in 275°F.

2 Cut prosciutto into ½-inch lengths and then crosswise to make ½-inch dice.

3 Place diced prosciutto onto baking sheet lined with parchment and bake until just crisped, firm and slightly caramelized. Remove from the oven and let cool to room temperature.

4 Toss greens with Smokey Tomato Vinaigrette and pinch of kosher salt and freshly ground black pepper.

5 Sprinkle with crisped prosciutto and julienne of red onion.

6 Layer mozzarella and sliced tomatoes over dressed greens and drizzle with a little additional vinaigrette.

GULF SHRIMP SALAD

WITH WAKAME, MACADAMIA NUTS

AND SLIVERED TROPICAL FRUIT

SERVES 4

Spicy Thai Peanut Vinaigrette (see page 230)

6 cups mixed greens (We use mâche, frisée and arugula greens and buckwheat, sunflower and pea shoots and whatever else looks best at the market.)

Kosher salt

Freshly ground black pepper

Thinly sliced dried pineapple, mango and peach and other dried tropical fruit

¼ cup macadamia nuts, toasted and crushed

¼ cup dried unsweetened coconut shavings

¾ cup wakame seaweed*

12 Spicy Gulf Shrimp (recipe follows)

1 Toss greens with vinaigrette and a pinch of kosher salt and freshly ground black pepper.

2 Place greens on chilled plate and sprinkle with dried fruit, coconut shavings and macadamia nuts. Add a dollop of wakame and finally 3 gulf shrimp per salad.

SPICY GULF SHRIMP

12 jumbo gulf shrimp, peeled and deveined, tail left on

1–2 tablespoons extra virgin olive oil

Kosher salt

Freshly ground black pepper

2 teaspoons fresh garlic, minced

⅓ cup good quality dry white wine

2–3 tablespoons Tiger Sauce to taste

⅓ cup Fresh Herb Butter (see page 33)

1 Season shrimp generously with kosher salt and freshly ground black pepper, add shrimp to pan and sauté on one side until pink. Turn shrimp over and add garlic, sauté briefly.

2 Deglaze with wine, then add Tiger Sauce and toss well to combine.

3 When shrimp is just cooked through, finish with Fresh Herb Butter – toss well again and remove from heat while still slightly creamy. Adjust seasonings generously to taste.

*Available at most Asian markets, gourmet grocers or even grocery store sushi counters.

STIR FRIED CURED DUCK SALAD
WITH SPICY ROASTED SWEET POTATOES,
CARAMELIZED APPLES AND PEARS

SERVES 4

This salad is perfect in the autumn and winter – which is generally when TR Durham stockpiles his Cured Duck Breast Prosciutto to get us through the Michigan winter. If you get some of his duck breast prosciutto, make sure to reserve the fat, which develops an incredible flavor through the curing process – render it and use it to sauté everything from potatoes to haricots verts.

Spicy Roasted Sweet Potatoes (see page 154)
1 tablespoon salted butter
1 tablespoon plus 1 teaspoon light oil
1 Granny Smith apple, sliced into about 8 wedges
1 ripe pear, sliced into about 8 wedges
½ cup Brown Sugar Spice (see page 242) or golden brown sugar
Chateau de Stony Muscat or your favorite Muscat

6 ounces cured duck breast, thinly sliced*
3 tablespoons unsalted cold butter
12 Baby Bibb lettuce leaves
½–¾ cup Sweet Fig Vinaigrette (see page 230)
¼ cup additional Brown Sugar Spice to taste, (see page 242) or golden brown sugar

1   Heat 1 tablespoon butter and 1 tablespoon plus 1 teaspoon light oil in one large or two medium non-reactive pans over medium heat.

2   Sear apples and pears in 1 tablespoon each light oil and butter until golden – add ¼–½ cup Brown Sugar Spice and sauté until lightly caramelized and just tender but still holds shape.

3   Deglaze with Chateau de Stony, add Spicy Roasted Sweet Potatoes, sliced duck and cold butter – toss together and then remove from heat.

4   To serve, arrange a few leaves of Bib lettuce on each plate – mound duck, apple, and sweet potato mixture onto plate tucked into the center of the greens.

5   Drizzle lettuce leaves with Sweet Fig Vinaigrette and sprinkle with a little additional Brown Sugar Spice.

*Available through Durham Tracklements, see sources, page 248.

MAIN COURSE

This is not a list of basic cooking techniques – like how to sear, sauté, sweat, roast or braise – but little things which I think can make a real difference in the results you get – whatever you are cooking. They are not actually difficult, just a matter of taking the time – maybe a few extra seconds – and being into what you are doing. If you do these things properly and consistently, your food will be at a different level. Cooking thoughtfully and with attention to detail is as much an approach to cooking, as it is a matter of precise technique.

Season evenly and generously – Every bite of an ingredient, notwithstanding textural differences, should taste the same – you don't want to bite into a salty bite and then a peppery bite and then a bland one. It is worth it to take an extra few seconds when seasoning your ingredients to get this consistency. If you season by raising your hand a slight distance above the food as you season it, you will get more even distribution and therefore, more even taste. If you season your food generously in advance of cooking, the salt will be able to penetrate deeper and become more integrated with the ingredient as it cooks, bringing out the maximum flavor of the ingredient itself as opposed to seasoning after an ingredient has been cooked which will leave a one-dimensional salty layer over the shell that has been created during the cooking process.

We make and cook with a lot of spice mixtures at the restaurant, but we always season first with salt, then with pepper and last with the spice mixture so the spice mixture won't create a barrier to the salt penetrating the ingredient and allowing the salt to bring out the most and best flavor of the ingredient as it cooks. At the restaurant, we consistently use kosher salt and freshly ground black pepper. We never use iodized salt as it has a harsh, aggressive taste and is made up of tiny, rock-hard granules, neither of which you really want to contribute to your food. Kosher salt generally comes in the form of a flatter flake which dissolves easily into food and also has a more delicate and natural taste. Sea salt is also a softer salt both in form and flavor – it melts easily into food and has a beautiful and gentle range of flavors, but is somewhat distinctive, and when you are not trying to add an additional flavor, but bring out the true flavor of your ingredients, kosher salt is, I think, the best (we use Diamond brand). There is a different world between buying ground pepper or simply grinding pepper as needed from a peppermill. You can branch out and experiment with all of the varieties of peppercorns – Telicherry, Malabar, Sarawak, green, white – learn about how they are harvested and notice all of the differences in taste, but any basic fresh, black peppercorn freshly ground will blow away a commercially packaged ground jar of pepper and is definitely worth the small effort or expense.

When sautéing or searing, place your ingredient presentation side down in a hot pan – move it once to allow oil to slip under it so it won't stick and then leave it alone until it is ready to be turned – The first side that you place in a pan will generally come out in the most pristine condition, as the pan is the cleanest during this portion of the cooking process – and so should be your presentaton side. Following this process will consistently bring you the most beautiful results.

Taste thoughtfully – Use your senses and don't rush – be open-minded and see where it leads you.

Pay attention to texture and contrast – Something complex, spicy or earthy will always benefit from something cool, clean or bright as a complement. This refreshes your palate and brings out the best of both tastes.

Don't give up easily – You can fix a lot of things if you remain calm and don't give up right away.

Don't take shortcuts that compromise the quality – It is better to simplify a recipe or take out some components than to do technique hastily.

For large batches, make a test before cooking the entire batch – For example, if you are making a big batch of Conch Fritters, Vietnamese Sausage or Turkey Burgers – take a small amount and cook it individually to taste how the whole batch will come out – adjust the batch and repeat the process. This only takes a couple of minutes, but prevents the whole batch from coming out less than ideally.

Choose the right sized pan – So that the food you are cooking will have enough room to sear and caramelize properly, instead of being crowded and essentially steam in its own juices. As ingredients caramelize they develop flavor and texture and along with controlling the heat, choosing the right size pan is the best way to ideally caramelize and thus, flavor your food.

Adjust your heat – It is difficult to prescribe in writing what the ideal heat is for cooking a particular item. If you pay attention to how your food is reacting to the heat as you cook, you can quickly learn to adjust to the subtleties of cooking and master the art of controlling your heat.

Don't follow a recipe blindly – When you are really paying attention to the look, feel and taste of the food, you have the best chance of getting the most delicious results. There are a lot of intangible factors like the season or quality or condition of the ingredients you are working with that can have a great effect on any given recipe and may not have been taken into account in writing the recipe. The combination of the idea for a dish in a recipe combined with being really into what you are doing, is the best chance for creating something special.

Choose the right oil – When cooking over high heat for an extended period of time, a pure, light cooking oil such as peanut, safflower or canola is ideal. Many people will advise you never to cook with extra virgin olive oil because it burns at a lower temperature than a pure, light cooking oil. However, for searing quick-cooking ingredients I think it actually helps to develop a deeper, richer color and unctuous quality in the food. While you do lose some of the subtle flavor of the oil, it really helps to develop a beautiful crispiness along with a depth of flavor you wouldn't get from cooking with lighter oil. Reserve the most special, complex extra virgin olive oil to be savored raw and simply. Other full-flavored oils and fat can make a great contribution to your food, like walnut oil, which contributes a nutty, earthy and pleasantly bitter flavor, or duck fat which contributes a smokey, earthy flavor and unsurpassable richness to a dish.

Be organized – For me, getting organized allows me the freedom to be free-spirited in my cooking. If I start with a clean workspace and have all of my things in place (Mise en Place) when I begin, I can really concentrate on the ingredients I am working with. Using proper technique when cooking is the next extension of this – when something is cooked properly, it gives you the ability to adjust to any unpredictable glitches that might arise – there is less room for error and a better chance for good results. Using proper technique is a basic structure that gives you a cushion to adjust to anything that comes up – it puts your best foot forward as well as providing you skills you can apply to anything you cook in the future.

SERVES 4

The ideal time to make this dish is in September through October when the equally brief seasons for pomegranates and New England swordfish coincide and both are at their prime. It is made up of an unusual amalgamation of flavors and textures that, I think, work really well together.

Four 7-ounce steaks New England swordfish
Kosher salt
Freshly ground black pepper
Miso Brown Sugar Rub (see page 245) – (You will have this remaining from making Miso Lemon Grass Oil.)
Miso Lemon Grass Oil, one batch (see page 236)
1 cup Guava Citrus Vinaigrette (see page 229)

1½ cups sea beans*
¼ cup Ikura (salmon roe)**
¼ cup pomegranate seeds, (Pomegranates do have a limited season, but are generally available September through December.)
Coconut Ginger Rice, one batch (see page 147)

1   Season both sides of swordfish with kosher salt and freshly ground black pepper.

2   Rub swordfish with Miso Brown Sugar Rub and let sit for minimum of 20 minutes and up to 2 hours.

3   Heat Miso Lemon Grass Oil in a non-reactive poaching pot with rack or a wide, shallow, braising pan about 4–6 inches deep to a bare simmer and place swordfish side by side gently into oil. Fish should be submerged in oil and not overlapping.

4   Allow swordfish to poach gently for a minimum of 20 minutes and up to 45 minutes. Fish will continue to get more tender and more succulent as it continues to cook.

5   While fish is poaching, toss sea beans, salmon roe and pomegranate seeds with some Guava Citrus Vinaigrette, lightly seasoning with kosher salt and freshly ground pepper to taste.

6   Just before removing fish, mound rice in center of plate – sprinkle sea bean mixture around rice and spoon a little additional Guava Citrus Vinaigrette onto plate. Remove fish gently and place over rice.

Available at specialty markets, like Whole Foods markets, see sources, page 248.
**Available at most Asian Markets and seafood markets.*

MACADAMIA ENCRUSTED SALMON

SERVES 4

Four 7-ounce pieces salmon filets
Kosher salt
Freshly ground black pepper
Chili Mélange (see page 242)
Chili Mélange Seasoned Flour (see page 244)
Egg Wash (recipe follows)
Macadamia Nut Mix (recipe follows)
Light olive oil or light cooking oil

Lemon Scented Mayonnaise (see page 228)
Cilantro Lime Salsa (see page 222)
Coconut Ginger Rice, one batch (see page 147)
Vegetable of the season such as Sugar Snap Peas
    with Fresh Lime and Mint (see page 141)
    or Chopped and Sautéed Brussels Sprouts
    (see page 135)

1   Season salmon generously in the following order
    with kosher salt, freshly ground black pepper,
    and Chili Mélange.

2   Dredge in Chili Mélange Seasoned Flour and shake
    off excess.

3   Dip in Egg Wash.

4   Roll in Macadamia Nut Mix, patting to create a
    good crust.

5   Refrigerate for at least 15 minutes so crust will
    set up and adhere to salmon during cooking.

6   Preheat oven to 400°F.

7   Heat oil in large oven-proof sauté pan and sauté
    salmon over medium-low heat until salmon is toasted
    and golden being careful not to allow nuts to get
    too dark before coating has become deep golden
    throughout. Turn salmon and continue to cook
    salmon for a few minutes. Transfer salmon to
    oven until salmon is just cooked though, about
    10 minutes per inch thickness.

8   To serve, neatly mound rice in center of each plate –
    place salmon over rice and garnish with a small
    dollop each of Lemon Scented Mayonnaise and
    Cilantro Lime Salsa. Accompany with Sugar Snap
    Peas with Fresh Lime and Mint or your favorite
    vegetable of the season.

MACADAMIA NUT MIX

2 cups salted macadamia nuts
1 cup panko (Japanese breadcrumbs)
Kosher salt as needed depending on if you are
    using salted or unsalted macadamia nuts

Combine all by pulsing in food processor until
coarsely ground.

EGG WASH

3 eggs
¼ cup whipping cream or whole milk

Combine eggs with heavy cream or milk.

While fresh and summery, this dish also has a little bit of heat so beware!

12 large scallops, preferably dry scallops that have not been frozen or soaked or injected with saline
Chili Mélange (see page 242)
Chili Mélange Seasoned Flour (see page 244)
Light olive oil
1 pound fresh tagliatelle, cooked al dente in boiling salted water and tossed lightly in olive oil and set aside at room temperature
Extra virgin olive oil
¾ cup red onions, fine julienne
¼ cup garlic, minced
1¼ cups good quality, dry white wine

1 teaspoon extra hot sauce (we use Melinda's brand)
4 tablespoons hot sauce (we use Tiger brand)
2 cups greens, torn, such as baby arugula, Swiss chard, dandelion, beet or mustard greens
1 cup wakame seaweed*
Kosher salt
2 tablespoons extra-virgin olive oil, additional for finishing
Freshly ground black pepper
Black sesame seeds, optional

1   Prepare scallops by seasoning generously in the following order with kosher salt, freshly ground black pepper and Chili Mélange.

2   Dredge scallops in Chili Mélange Seasoned Flour and shake off excess.

3   Heat olive oil in large non-stick sauté pan over medium-high heat and sear scallops, being careful not to overcrowd or scallops will steam instead of caramelize – should take about two minutes per side. If you don't have a large enough pan to accommodate all the scallops, it is okay to cook scallops in batches and keep in warm place.

4   In a separate large sauté pan, heat olive oil over medium-high heat and sauté for about a minute, then add red onions and continue to sauté until soft and aromatic – season with kosher salt and freshly ground black pepper. Deglaze with white wine, bring to a simmer and cook for an additional minute or two.

5   Add Melinda's and Tiger Sauce, cooking for an additional minute and add greens and wakame, pasta, and then additional extra-virgin olive oil – toss well to combine and adjust seasonings generously.

6   To serve, spoon pasta into large shallow bowls, sprinkle with black sesame seeds and arrange scallops over top.

Available at most Asian markets, gourmet grocers or even grocery store sushi counters.

IF YOU DO NOT FEEL IT – YOU WILL NEVER FEEL IT

When I was studying at Le Cordon Bleu, there was one teacher in particular, Chef Christian, who was everybody's favorite. He was light-hearted and easy mannered – he was the cool, laid back teacher. Every day in his class he would pass out beautiful cookbooks from his collection for everyone to look at. He was always joking around and was friends with all of the students.

One day, about six months into the program, a student raised his hand asking for the recipe for crème anglaise. Chef Christian shouted incredulously (with a strong French accent) "The recipe? The recipe?! IF YOU DO NOT FEEL IT – YOU WILL NEVER FEEL IT!" We had just gone through six months of intense training, being instructed to follow each recipe to a tee – which was a new experience for me because that is not how I had learned to cook. I guess it was a matter of balance – now that we knew the basic technique – Le base – it was time to really pay attention to the food – not to rely on the recipe alone. It wasn't that it was wrong to use a recipe, but one shouldn't rely on it blindly – to look at the food – taste it carefully, paying attention to the color – the consistency and body. When Chef Christian shouted, "If you do not feel it, you will never feel it" so passionately, it seemed to express a whole outlook towards cooking.

Just living in a city and a country where food is such an important part of the culture – walking through the markets – being around chefs who were that dead serious about the food made more of an impression on me than any of the recipes or even the techniques. I am not sure exactly what he meant – I think everyone in the room kind of got the idea and interpreted it in their own way – he was so genuinely passionate in saying it.

In our kitchen, sometimes one of the staff will burst out with "If you do not feel it, you will never feel it" – probably because I have told them the story so many times to make a point. But I think if something is there, it is there – it is just natural, and that is the most important thing. Either you are into the food or you're not – it doesn't matter where you went to school, or what terms or recipes you have memorized. At The Restaurant, one thing that I am confident of is that everybody just really cares about the food, about the welfare of the restaurant and the customers and each other – and that is a very good feeling –

SEAFOOD LASAGNA
WITH CRISPED PROSCIUTTO DI PARMA

SERVES 4

I can't lie – this may be tied with the Moroccan Chicken for most labor-intensive recipe, but on the plus side, many of the components can be prepared in advance and it is also one of the most requested recipes from our customers.

3 fresh lasagna sheets, cut into 8 squares
   (about 4 x 6 inches each)*
Light olive oil
Steamed Mussels (recipe follows)
Sautéed Shrimp and Scallops (recipe follows)
6–8 cups Tomato Cream, one batch (see page 223)
½ cup aged Parmigiano Reggianno, shredded

2 cups fresh mozzarella, sliced
½ cup herbed goat cheese
1½ cups fresh spinach
8 tablespoons proscuitto, minced

Crisped Prosciutto, for garnish (recipe follows)

1 Preheat oven to 375°F.

2 Bring large pot of salted water to a boil. Meanwhile prepare an ice bath by mixing 2 cups of ice with cold water in a large bowl.

3 Blanch pasta squares in boiling water for one to two seconds, then immediately submerge in ice bath.

4 Dry pasta gently with a clean kitchen towel – set aside separately so that they do not stick. Brush lightly with olive oil to prevent pasta from drying out.

5 These lasagnas are individual, so assemble each lasagna on an oven-proof plate or a lightly greased sheet tray.

6 On each oven-proof plate, place a small pool of Tomato Cream to use as a bed for the pasta.

7 Place one sheet of pasta over Tomato Cream.

8 Spoon a small amount of Tomato Cream – about ¼ cup to cover pasta.

9 Place a small handful of fresh spinach over Tomato Cream.

10 Place shrimp, scallops and mussels in a bundle over spinach, distributing evenly among the 4 lasagnas.

11 Place 6–8 mussels on top of shrimp and scallops.

12 Crumble about 2 tablespoons herbed goat cheese over seafood.

13 Place a slice of fresh mozzarella over goat cheese layer.

14 Sprinkle light layer of shredded Parmigiano Regianno cheese.

15 Place a small amount of diced prosciutto over cheese.

16 Spread enough Tomato Cream to cover seafood.

17 Top with one more sheet of pasta.

18 Spread small amount of Tomato Cream over pasta, making sure edges are not covered so they can brown up nicely during cooking.

19 Top with a slice of fresh mozzarella.

20 Place in oven and bake for 15–20 minutes, or until pasta edges are crisp and center of lasagna is hot.

21 Remove from oven and top with crisped prosciutto.

32 mussels, about 1½ pounds
2 tablespoons fresh garlic, minced
2 tablespoons shallots, minced
2 fresh thyme sprig
½ cup good quality, dry white wine
Light olive oil

1 Place mussels in an ice bath, swirl around and discard any mussels that do not close up – drain well.

2 Sauté garlic, shallots, salt, pepper, and a few sprigs of thyme in olive oil in large, wide non-reactive pot.

3 Add mussels, stir, sauté for a few minutes and add white wine to deglaze – cover pot, shaking often until mussels open (about 5 minutes). Remove from heat when most mussels open.

4 Remove from heat and when cool enough to handle remove mussels from shells and discard shells. You will not need the resulting cooking liquid in this recipe but it makes a delicious broth for a soup or other use. Set mussels aside at room temperature for assembly.

These can be prepared up to a day in advance and refrigerated until lasagna is ready for assembly.

12 shrimp, peeled and deveined
8 large scallops, preferably dry scallops that have not been frozen or soaked or injected with saline
2 tablespoons fresh garlic, minced
Light olive oil
3 tablespoons Fresh Herb Butter (see page 33)
Light olive oil

1 Sauté garlic in olive oil until fragrant in large non-reactive pan.

2 Place shrimp and scallops in pan, season with salt and pepper and sauté for another couple of minutes until barely cooked. Add Fresh Herb Butter and toss to coat, Herb Butter should be just melted, but remain creamy.

3 Transfer seafood onto a cutting board and when cool enough to handle cut shrimp and scallops in half or in big chunks. Keep at room temperature for assembly.

These can be prepared up to a day in advance and stored covered at room temperature.

4 thin slices Prosciutto di Parma

1 Preheat oven to 275°F.

2 Lay prosciutto on sheet tray lined with parchment. Place in oven for about 10 minutes, or until prosciutto has just dried out and is toasty and fragrant.

3 Remove from heat and let cool to room temperature.

*Available at most gourmet grocers.

SEAFOOD LASAGNA

WITH CRISPED

PROSCIUTTO DI PARMA

SEARED SCALLOPS
WITH MANGO CREAM AND EXOTIC FRUIT CHUTNEY

SERVES 4

16–20 large scallops, preferably dry scallops that have not been frozen or soaked or injected with saline
¼ cup Chili Mélange (see page 242)
½ cup Chili Mélange Seasoned Flour (see page 244)
Kosher salt, generously to taste
Freshly ground black pepper, to taste
1–2 tablespoons olive oil

Coconut Ginger Rice, one batch (see page 147)
Mango Cream (see page 216)
Exotic Fruit Chutney (see page 219)
Vegetable of the season such as Spring Vegetable Mélange (see page 146), or Chopped and Sautéed Brussels Sprouts (see page 135)

1   Prepare scallops by seasoning generously in the following order with kosher salt, freshly ground black pepper and Chili Mélange.

2   Dredge scallops in Chili Mélange Seasoned Flour and shake off excess.

3   Heat olive oil in large non-stick sauté pan over medium-high heat and sear scallops, being careful not to overcrowd or scallops will steam instead of caramelize – should take about two minutes per side. If you don't have a large enough pan to accommodate all the scallops, it is okay to cook scallops in batches and keep warm.

4   To serve, mound rice in center of each plate – spoon Mango Cream onto plate surrounding rice. Distribute scallops evenly around sauce and place small bundles of vegetables between each scallop – garnish with a dollop of Exotic Fruit Chutney.

WHOLE GRILLED LOUP DE MER
STUFFED WITH CREOLE RATATOUILLE

SERVES 4

4 whole loup de mer (also known as European sea bass)*, cleaned and de-boned – fish monger can prepare for you or four 6 ounce filets of your favorite fish
Kosher salt, to taste
Freshly ground black pepper, to taste

Chili Mélange, to taste (see page 242)
½ cup herbed goat cheese
2 cups Creole Ratatouille (see page 135)
12–16 grape leaves, lightly rinsed and dried**
Extra virgin olive oil
Grill basket

1 Heat grill to medium-high.

2 Prepare fish by seasoning generously with kosher salt, lightly with freshly ground black pepper and Chili Mélange (in that order – make sure to season cavity of fish generously as well as outside). If using filets season and then proceed with recipe.

3 Fill cavity of fish with Creole Ratatouille and two tablespoons of herbed goat cheese in center.

4 Rinse grape leaves briefly in cool water and pat dry – lay flat on cutting board, overlapping leaves to twice the size of the fish.

5 Place fish near one edge of grape leaves, with head and tail exposed, and roll up entire fish tightly in leaves. Repeat with remaining 3 fish.

6 Brush extremely lightly with extra virgin olive oil and place fish in grill basket (if you don't have a grill basket, tie with butcher's twine to hold fish together).

7 Grill for about 20 minutes, turning halfway (tastes great over charcoal or wood).

*Available at Monahan's Seafood Market, see sources, page 248.
*Available at ZZ's Market, see sources, page 248.

FLASH-FRIED LAKE PERCH ROLLED IN CORNMEAL WITH MANGO CREAM, SPICY COLESLAW AND BUTTERMILK BISCUITS

SERVES 4

2 pounds lake perch
3 quarts light cooking oil for frying
Kosher salt
Freshly ground black pepper
2 cups buttermilk
4 cups Spiced Cornmeal (see page 244)

Mango Cream (see page 216)
Buttermilk Biscuits (see page 212), made just prior to serving
Guava Butter (see page 33)
Spicy Coleslaw (see page 133)

1   Heat oil in electric fryer or heavy pot to 350°F.

2   Season perch evenly with kosher salt and freshly ground pepper.

3   Place buttermilk and Spiced Cornmeal separately into two shallow dishes.

4   Dip perch first into buttermilk and then immediately dredge in Spiced Cornmeal Mixture. Shake off excess cornmeal.

5   Flash fry lake perch until crisp golden and just cooked through.

6   To serve, spoon a pool of Mango Cream in the center. Place fish in center of sauce and surround with biscuit topped with Guava Butter and bundle of Spicy Coleslaw.

ROASTED POBLANOS
STUFFED WITH CURRIED SHRIMP, SCALLOPS AND ANDOUILLE SAUSAGE

SERVES 6

These Poblanos may be prepared up to one day in advance, though you will want to bring them to room temperature before baking.

3 poblanos, split in half lengthwise, ribs and seeds removed
3 tablespoons extra virgin olive oil
Light olive oil for cooking
1 tablespoon salted butter
1 cup onion, finely diced
1 tablespoon plus 1 teaspoon garlic, minced
1 tablespoon plus 1 teaspoon ginger, minced
½ jalapeño, seeded and minced
1 teaspoon Curry Spice (see page 234)*
2 teaspoons Chili Mélange (see page 242)
4 jumbo gulf shrimp, peeled and deveined, finely chopped
5 large sea scallops, preferably dry scallops that have not been frozen or soaked or injected with saline, finely chopped

⅓ cup andouille, or Cajun sausage, small dice
¾–1 cup smoked mozzarella, shredded
⅓ cup scallions, green and white parts (remove tough ends)
1 heaping tablespoon chopped cilantro
1 heaping tablespoon chopped parsley
1 teaspoon firmly packed brown sugar
1 teaspoon sriracha (we use Shark brand)**
Kosher salt
Freshly ground black pepper

Carrot Lime Purée (see page 226)
Crème Fraîche (see page 231)
Coconut Ginger Rice, one batch (see page 147)

1 Preheat oven to 425°F.

2 Drizzle halved poblanos with olive oil and kosher salt, lay out on sheet tray and roast in oven for about 10–12 minutes until tender. Remove and set aside.

3 Sweat onions, garlic, ginger and jalapeños for about 3 minutes on medium-low heat with butter and olive oil in a large non-reactive sauté pan. Season with kosher salt, freshly ground black pepper, Curry Spice and Chili Mélange.

4 Add seafood and sausage and sauté until the seafood just loses translucency.

5 Remove from heat and transfer to large mixing bowl – add green onion, cilantro, parsley, brown sugar, and sriracha.

6 Adjust seasonings generously to taste.

7 Divide stuffing between 6 poblano halves – sprinkle with shredded smoked mozzarella and bake in 425°F oven for about 15 minutes until mozzarella is golden and bubbly and seafood mixture is hot in center.

8 Serve each poblano topped with a dollop of Carrot Lime Purée and then Crème Fraîche and accompany with Coconut Ginger Rice.

Available through Penzeys, see sources, page 248.
**Available at most Asian markets.*

8 large sea scallops, preferably dry scallops that have not been frozen or soaked or injected with saline
12 jumbo gulf shrimp, peeled and deveined with tails left on
Extra virgin olive oil
¾ cup red onion, fine julienne
1 cup sugar snap peas, fine julienne

Kosher salt, to taste
Freshly ground black pepper, to taste
4 cups Curry Cream, one batch (see page 217)
1 pound fresh pasta – cooked until al dente in boiling, salted water and tossed with a small amount of extra virgin olive oil, torn or cut into ribbons*
2 cups fresh baby spinach
½ cup shredded Parmigiano Reggiano or aged provolone, additional for garnish

1 Season shrimp and scallops with kosher salt and freshly ground black pepper and set aside.

2 Heat oil in a large sauté pan and sauté shrimp and scallops over medium-high heat until just cooked through, being careful not to overcrowd pan or seafood will not be able to caramelize properly – and set aside.

3 While seafood is cooking, in separate sauté pan, heat olive oil and sauté onions for 1–2 minutes – add sugar snap peas, toss and cook very briefly, about 30 seconds. Season with kosher salt and freshly ground black pepper.

4 Add Curry Cream and bring to a simmer and adjust seasoning generously to taste.

5 Add pasta to Curry Cream and toss until evenly coated – adjust seasonings to taste.

6 To serve, make a small ruffle of baby spinach around perimeter of each bowl, mound pasta in the center and top with shredded Reggiano and sautéed shrimp and scallops.

*Available at most gourmet grocers and Pastabilities.

This is another very simple, but extremely versatile preparation that you will see throughout our recipes – from Spicy Roast Sweet Potatoes to Curried Soft Shell Crabs, to Moroccan Scallops. Once you get this simple seasoning technique down, you can mix and match various spice blends and come up with your own combinations.

4 servings of fish, whole or filleted
Chili Mélange (see page 242)
Chili Mélange Seasoned Flour (see page 244)
Kosher salt, generously to taste
Freshly ground black pepper, to taste
Light olive oil
Freshly squeezed lime juice

Cilantro Lime Salsa (see page 222)
Coconut Ginger Rice (see page 147)
Vegetables of the season such as Cool Thai
    Cucumbers (see page 132) or Spring Vegetable
    Mélange (see page 146)

1   Preheat oven to 400°F.

2   Heat oil in non-stick pan.

3   While oil is heating, prepare fish by seasoning generously in the following order with kosher salt, freshly ground black pepper and Chili Mélange.

4   Dredge fish in Chili Mélange Seasoned Flour and shake off excess.

5   Place fish, presentation side down, in hot pan – sear until golden, turn over, and place in oven until fish is just cooked – fish will have just lost its translucency – should take about 10 minutes per inch thickness of fish.

6   Finish by dressing fish with freshly squeezed lime juice and serve with Coconut Ginger Rice, Cilantro Lime Salsa and favorite vegetable of the season (see accompaniments pages 132–154).

MICHIGAN RABBIT
BRAISED IN CÉPE CREAM WITH POLENTA BISCUITS
AND ROASTED FARMER'S MARKET CARROTS

SERVES 4

This is a pretty decadent dish – Cépes may not always be available, and buying them fresh is somewhat of a splurge – so feel free to substitute your favorite mushrooms or even just to season the sauce with a handful of the precious cépes. We have made this sauce with almost every combination of mushrooms you could think of and it is always delicious.

2 whole rabbits
Kosher salt
Freshly ground black pepper
Chili Mélange (see page 242)
Chili Mélange Seasoned Flour (see page 244)
4 quarts Cépe Cream, one batch (see page 217)

Roasted Farmer's Market Carrots (see page 143)
Polenta Biscuits (see page 211)

1   Cut each rabbit into 5 pieces (4 legs + saddle).

2   Season rabbit generously with kosher salt, freshly ground black pepper, and lightly with Chili Mélange.

3   Dredge in Chili Mélange Seasoned Flour and shake off excess.

4   Brown rabbit in olive oil over medium-high heat until just golden – remove from pan immediately, but do not discard pan – pour off excess oil.

5   Add Cépe Cream to pan, reserving 1 quart for dressing the rabbit just before serving – Stir to incorporate caramelized bits into sauce and bring to a gentle simmer.

6   Gently place rabbit into sauce – the sauce should come to ¾ way up the rabbit – spoon some sauce over the rabbit to coat it.

7   Bring to a low simmer and cover with tightly sealed lid (Le Creuset casserole pans are ideal) or cover tightly with professional grade film wrap, and then foil and place in 250°F oven.

8   Cook until rabbit is extremely tender and almost falling off the bone – about 3½ hours.

9   Remove the rabbit and either add additional sauce to thicken and deepen the flavor, or remove braising liquid/sauce to make into soup, and bring fresh sauce to a simmer.

10 Adjust seasoning and dress the rabbit with sauce.

11 Finish with chopped fresh herbs.

12 Serve rabbit dressed with additional Cépe Cream. Accompany with Roasted Farmer's Market Carrots and Polenta Biscuits.

SERVES 4

This is the dish I made for my final examination at Le Cordon Bleu and it generally appears somewhere on our menu – whether as a first course or an entrée. It is inspired by pastilla, or pigeon pie, the Moroccan dish traditionally eaten to break the daily fast of Ramadan. I love the combinations of sweet, spicy and savory ingredients that come together in this complex dish – it is definitely an all-day project (at least) but is worth the work. Even though I am generally not a big proponent of freezing things, this is one thing that freezes well and might encourage you to take it on.

1 tablespoon kosher salt

¼ teaspoon freshly ground black pepper

3½ pounds chicken, cut into 8 parts (if using chicken pieces – more dark than light meat is best)

¼ cup light olive oil

6 cups yellow onions, rough chop

2 tablespoons fresh garlic, minced

2 teaspoons fresh ginger, minced

½ teaspoon ground cloves

½ teaspoon ground ginger

1⅛ teaspoons ground turmeric

½ teaspoon cayenne

2 pinches saffron

2 cups water

2 eggs, lightly beaten

½ bunch cilantro, rough chop

¼ bunch fresh parsley, rough chop

⅛ bunch fresh mint, rough chop

½ teaspoon cinnamon

1 small cinnamon stick

Pinch of additional cayenne

¾ cup sliced almonds, toasted until golden in 350°F oven

⅛–¼ cup sugar (or more to taste)

1 tablespoon fresh mint, rough chop, or more to taste

1 tablespoon cilantro, rough chop, or more to taste

1 tablespoon flat leaf parsley, rough chop, or more to taste

½ package phyllo, thawed and covered with a towel to keep from drying out

Light olive oil

Confectioner's Sugar-Cinnamon Mixture (recipe follows)

Cilantro Lime Salsa (see page 222)

Candied Limes (recipe follows)

Spicy Greens (see page 140)

1 Season chicken with kosher salt and pepper, then brown in olive oil and remove from pan.

2 Heat olive oil in large braising pan, and sauté onions, garlic, and ginger with spices.

3 Add water, cilantro, parsley, mint, cinnamon and cinnamon stick.

4 Add chicken back into pan and simmer until very tender and most of the liquid has evaporated – about 45 minutes to 1 hour, adding a little bit of water as needed. Pull chicken off the bone as it cooks, incorporating it into the mixture.

5 When chicken is extremely tender, remove chicken mixture from pan and place in large mixing bowl (reserve pan for next step – do not rinse).

6 Add eggs to hot pan and stir briskly until thickened but not set – may have to move on and off a low flame, being careful not to let eggs scramble.

7 Once chicken has cooled enough to handle, carefully remove all bones and the cinnamon stick.

8 Add thickened eggs, ½ cup of the toasted almonds, sugar, cilantro, parsley, mint and additional pinch of cayenne to chicken.

9 Adjust seasonings generously to taste – should be very flavorful, sweet and spicy – let mixture cool to room temperature.

10 Cut phyllo sheet into quarters. Layer three strips of phyllo brushing each lightly with olive oil and place a heaping ½ cup of filling in center. Roll tightly into a small package.

11 Bake with packages seam side down on lightly greased baking sheet in 375°F oven until crisp and golden – about 20 minutes.

12 To serve, dust with Confectioner's Sugar-Cinnamon Mixture and sprinkle with remaining ¼ cup toasted almonds. Accompany with Cilantro Lime Salsa, Candied Limes, and Spicy Greens.

CONFECTIONER'S SUGAR-CINNAMON MIXTURE

⅓ **cup confectioner's sugar**
½ **teaspoon good quality cinnamon**

Mix well to combine.

CANDIED LIMES

3 **cups water**
4 **cups brown sugar**
1–2 **pieces star anise**
3 **limes, sliced in ¼-inch slices**

1 Blanch limes three times very gently by placing into a large, non-reactive pot of cold water and bringing water up to just below a light simmer (strain and repeat two additional times handling the limes with great care as to not disturb the pulp).

2 Make simple syrup by combining brown sugar and water, bringing to a boil and then reducing to a bare simmer.

3 Place limes gently into syrup and poach at a shiver (just below a simmer). Cover with piece of parchment and poach until candied – about 2 hours.

4 Chill until ready to use.

PAILLARD OF CHICKEN
WITH FRESH PASTA, TOMATOES, BASIL AND BRIE

SERVES 4

4 medium ripe Roma tomatoes
½ cup fresh basil chiffonade, (ribbon cut)
¼ cup extra virgin olive oil
Four 6-ounce boneless chicken breasts, pounded
   to ¼-inch paillard
Kosher salt
Freshly ground black pepper
Chili Mélange (see page 242)
Chili Mélange Seasoned Flour (see page 244)
Light olive oil

½ cup Parmigiano Reggiano, grated (or other
   good quality parmesan)
1½ pounds favorite pasta, fresh or dried
2 tablespoons fresh garlic, minced
¾ pounds Brie or other soft, washed rind aromatic
   cheese such as Camembert or Talleggio
1½ teaspoons kosher salt
Freshly ground black pepper

1 Combine tomatoes, basil and olive oil and let sit at room temperature for at least 2 hours to allow flavors to meld together.

2 Bring large pot of salted water to a boil and reduce the heat to keep it hot, but not at a boil until needed.

3 Heat olive oil in a non-stick pan.

4 While oil is heating, prepare chicken by seasoning generously in the following order with kosher salt, freshly ground black pepper and Chili Mélange.

5 Dredge chicken in Seasoned Flour and shake off excess.

6 Place chicken in hot pan – sear until golden being careful not to overcrowd or chicken will steam instead of caramelize. Cook about half way, turn over and finish cooking, about 3 minutes per side.

7 While chicken is cooking – cook pasta in boiling salted water until al dente. Strain well and toss with tomato-basil-Brie mixture. Adjust seasoning generously to taste.

8 To serve, spoon pasta into shallow bowls, sprinkle with grated Reggiano and lay paillard of chicken over pasta.

SWEET AND SPICY MOULARD DUCK BREAST
WITH POTATO LATKES AND SPIKED APPLESAUCE

SERVES 4

This dish has a lot of really flavorful components that taste great together, but could also easily be paired down and still be delicious – pick and choose which you want to make. The marinated duck alone is delicious with the simplest accompaniments

4 Moulard duck breasts*
2 cups Aromatic Asian Marinade (see page 227)
Kosher salt
Freshly ground black pepper
Light cooking oil

Potato Latkes (see page 152)
Spiked Applesauce (see page 141) (made in advance
    and held at room temperature)
Crème Fraîche (see page 231) optional
Vegetable of the season – the simplest sautéed
    vegetables would be ideal for this dish such as
    Sugar Snap Peas with Fresh Lime and Mint (see
    page 141) or Haricots Verts Sautéed in Duck Fat
    (see page 138)

1 Marinate duck breast overnight (or up to 3 days) tossing well to distribute marinade evenly.

2 Preheat oven to 375°F.

3 Remove from marinade and wipe away excess marinade or sugars will scorch.

4 Season with kosher salt and freshly ground black pepper. Sear duck breasts fat side down on oven-proof sauté pan over medium heat until skin becomes crisp and golden. Turn duck over and place in oven to finish – should take about five minutes to reach medium rare. Simultaneously, or just in advance, fry latkes and remove to paper towel to absorb excess oil.

5 Serve duck with Potato Latkes topped with Spiked Applesauce and Crème Fraîche and simple vegetable of the season.

*Available through D'artagnan, see sources, page 248.

2–3½ pounds chickens, or 2 Poussin or 4 quail
2 quarts Thai BBQ Marinade (see page 227)
Kosher salt
Freshly ground black pepper

Cilantro Lime Salsa (see page 222)
Aromatic Spiced Orzo (see page 144)
Vegetables of the season such as Spring Vegetable
  Mélange (see page 146), Roast Farmer's Market
  Carrots (see page 143) or Sugar Snap Peas with
  Fresh Lime and Mint (see page 141)

1 Marinate chicken in 4 cups (1 quart) marinade
   for 24–36 hours.

2 In non-reactive, stainless steel saucepan place
   remaining 4 cups marinade and reduce over
   low heat until thickened.

3 Remove chicken from marinade and season
   generously with kosher salt and freshly ground
   black pepper.

4 Brush generously with reduced sauce and roast until
   just cooked through – internal temperature should
   rise above 150°F when checked with a thermometer.

5 Dress with Cilantro Lime Salsa and accompany
   with Aromatic Spiced Orzo Beans and vegetables
   of the season.

BRAISED BERKSHIRE PORK WITH AROMATIC SPICES

SERVES 4

This is even better re-warmed gently in the braising liquid the next day – and the leftovers also make great sandwiches with sliced avocado and melted, smoked mozzarella. You can use any high-quality pork available where you live, but it is worth it to splurge at least once and try some of the breed specific pork available at a local farm or through Heritage Foods – like Berkshire or Red Wattle – you won't believe the difference!

Braised Pork (recipe follows)
Warm Baguette, broken into big chunks

Gingered Sweet Potato Gratin, one batch (optional – see page 151), baguettes alone make a nice accompaniment
Vegetable of the season such as Spring Vegetable Mélange (see page 146) or Spicy Coleslaw (see page 133)

BRAISED PORK

One half boneless Boston butt, about 3½–4 pounds (we use Berkshire Pork)*
Light cooking oil for searing
Braising Liquid (recipe follows)
Kosher salt
Freshly ground black pepper

1 Preheat oven to 250F°.

2 Season both sides of pork shoulder generously with kosher salt and freshly ground black pepper.

3 Heat oil in large roasting or braising pan, and brown both sides of pork.

4 Heat braising liquid to a gentle simmer. Place pork into liquid – pork should be about ¾ of the way covered by the braising liquid with the top of the pork peeking through.

5 Cover pan and place in oven for about 5–6 hours or until extremely tender. Check the pork a few times during cooking process to be sure the liquid does not rise above a gentle simmer and turn the pork over after 2 hours.

6 Break pork into large chunks and serve hot or allow to cool to room temperature in braising liquid.

7 Heap pork onto plate and accompany with crusty baguettes to sop up juices, gratin and vegetable of the season.

BRAISING LIQUID

3 cups sweet chili sauce (we use Mae Ploy brand)**
1 cup mango chutney (we use Major Grey Patak's brand)***
½ cup soy sauce (we use Kikkoman brand)
¼ cup stone ground whole grain mustard
½ cup garlic, minced
1 tablespoon Chili Mélange (see page 242)
2 tablespoons Chinese five spice
1 teaspoon freshly ground black pepper
⅓ cup hoisin sauce (we use Koon Chun brand)**
⅓ cup Asian style barbecue sauce (we use Koon Chun brand)**
1 teaspoon brown sugar
2 cups Chicken Essence (see page 68) stock or broth (If using canned broth, use College Inn brand.)

Combine all ingredients in large non-reactive mixing bowl.

Available through Heritage Foods, see sources, page 248.
**Available at most Asian markets.*
***Available at most Indian markets or gourmet grocers.*

ENTRECÔTE OF BEEF
WITH GORGONZOLA CREAM, ESCAROLE AND FRESH TOMATOES

SERVES 4

A delicious and more economical substitution would be sliced grilled marinated flank using same marinade.

4 10-ounce entrecôte or rib-eye steaks
40 Cloves of Garlic Marinade (see page 227)
3 cups Triple Blue Cheese Dressing (see page 231)
2 cups escarole, torn into bite size pieces – If you can't find escarole, baby arugula makes a nice, easily accessible alternative.
1 cup ripe tomatoes, medium dice

Gingered Sweet Potato Gratin, one batch (see page 151)
Vegetable of the Season such as Grilled Pencil-Thin Asparagus (see page 139) or Spring Vegetable Mélange (see page 146)

1 Marinate flank for minimum of 8 hours and up to 48 hours tossing well to distribute marinade evenly.

2 Heat grill to medium-high to high.

3 Remove steak from marinade wiping away excess marinade and season with kosher salt and freshly ground black pepper.

4 Grill to medium rare about 5 minutes per side – remove from grill and let rest lightly tented in aluminum foil.

5 Meanwhile, warm pan over medium heat – add Triple Blue Cheese dressing and then stir in escarole, tomatoes and cook until just hot but some chunks of Blue Cheese remain.

6 To serve, spoon sauce into wide shallow bowls, fan steak out over sauce and accompany with Gingered Sweet Potato Gratin and vegetables of the season.

BEEF TENDERLOIN WITH CHIMICHURRI FESTOONED WITH MICHIGAN CORN

SERVES 4

Skirt steak, sirloin of lamb or almost any full-flavored cut of meat goes well with these spices and flavors. We wait all year for Michigan corn to be in season, but when corn isn't available, we have sautéed a simple julienne of sugar snap peas, red onions and halved grape tomatoes as an accompaniment, which is equally good.

Four 8–9 ounces tournedos of beef tenderloin
Extra virgin olive oil
Kosher salt
Freshly ground black pepper
Chili Mélange (see page 242) (you will have
  some remaining)

2 cups Chimichurri Sauce (see page 222) at room
   temperature
4 cups Michigan corn, scraped from cob

1 Season tournedos by drizzling lightly with extra virgin olive oil and rubbing it gently around beef until glistening – season evenly and generously with kosher salt and freshly ground black pepper and heavily with Chili Mélange, patting it lightly into beef.

2 Heat olive oil in large oven-proof skillet over medium-high heat – sear beef – making sure you have enough room as not to crowd or meat will not be able to sear and therefore develop best texture and flavor as it caramelizes. Shift each piece shortly after placing in pan to ensure it doesn't stick and then allow the meat to cook undisturbed until seared and cooked about halfway – about 4 minutes. Turn beef over and allow to cook until medium rare, about 4 more minutes. If you want to cook further – place skillet in 400°F oven for a couple of additional minutes until it reaches desired level of doneness. Set beef aside to rest lightly tented in aluminum foil until ready to serve.

3 Heat extra virgin olive oil in pan and sauté corn briefly about 2–3 minutes. Keep firm and crisp – season with kosher salt and freshly ground black pepper.

4 To serve, spoon Chimichurri Sauce onto center of each plate. Place beef tournedos overlapping sauce and surround with Michigan corn.

INDIAN INSPIRED LAMB PASTRY
WITH GOLDEN RAISINS AND SWEET POTATOES

SERVES 4

The recipe for these pastries was developed by Brendan McCall, who was inspired by his travels to India and his love of the exotic.

Lamb filling (recipe follows)
Dough (recipe follows)
Light cooking oil

Fresh Mint Chutney (see page 218)
Crème Fraîche (see page 231)

Vegetable of the season such as Sugar Snap Peas with Fresh Lime and Mint (see page 141) or any other simple vegetable (see accompaniments, pages 132–154) – this dish has a lot of complex flavor and tastes best accompanied with something simple to highlight those flavors.

1   Assemble pastries, by separating dough into eight balls, and then rolling them each into a thin circle. Distribute the lamb filling evenly between the eight dough rounds and moisten the edge of each pastry with a little bit of water. Fold dough over filling and crimp to seal.

2   Fry in electric deep fryer or heavy pan with 2–3 inches of vegetable oil heated to 350°F until golden brown. Season pastries with kosher salt immediately as they are removed from the oil.

3   Serve with Fresh Mint Chutney, Crème Fraîche and vegetable of the season.

DOUGH

3   cups all-purpose flour
3   tablespoons clarified or melted butter
1   teaspoon salt
¾–1 cup hot water
Kosher salt, to taste

1   Combine the flour, butter and salt – rubbing the clumps between your fingers until it becomes a sandy consistency.

2   Add the water in stages and mix until the dough just comes together. Knead the dough for 10 minutes on a cutting board, add the remaining ¼ cup of water if the dough refuses to come together.

3   Allow to rest for 15 minutes, covered with a damp towel.

LAMB FILLING

¾ cup sweet potato, skinned and ¼-inch dice
1 teaspoon saffron soaked in ⅓ cup hot water
1 tablespoon ginger, minced
1 tablespoon garlic, minced
½ cup white onion, ¼-inch dice
1 pound finely chopped sirloin of lamb* or
    lean ground lamb
1½ teaspoons Garam Masala (see page 239)
½ teaspoon cayenne pepper
1 tablespoon plus 1 teaspoon whole cumin
1 heaping tablespoon brown sugar, or more
    to taste
4 ounces golden raisins soaked in Pommeau
    de Normande*, to just cover (Pommeau de
    Normande is a Calvados seasoned with apple
    juice – if you can't find,it where you live, use
    a combination of Calvados and apple cider.)
½ teaspoon kosher salt

1   Poach sweet potatoes in a shallow pan over low
    heat incorporating saffron water mixture.
    Cook until just soft.

2   Sauté ginger, garlic, and onions in oil a separate
    large sauté pan over moderate heat until translucent.
    Add the lamb and increase the heat to medium-high.
    Stir frequently, add sweet potato mixture and cook
    until liquid evaporates.

3   Add Garam Masala, cayenne, cumin, brown sugar
    and raisins. Cook for 5 minutes. Adjust seasonings
    generously and allow to cool to room temperature
    before assembling pastries.

*Available at Morgan and York, see sources, page 248.
**Available through D'atagnan, see sources, page 248.

SERVES 4

4 pork loin or large center cut pork chops
2 shallots, sliced
2 garlic cloves, sliced
3 tablespoons lemon grass, minced
1 teaspoon fish sauce
1 teaspoon soy sauce
¼ teaspoon salt
1 tablespoon sugar
1 tablespoon vegetable oil

Purée of Curried Roasted Sweet Potato Pumpkin and Apple (see page 232)
Pickled Local Apples (see page 134)
Gingered Sweet Potato Gratin, one batch (see page 151)
Spicy Greens (see page 140)

1   Preheat oven to 375°F.

2   Place the shallots and garlic in mortar and pestle or food processor and mash or purée into a paste.

3   Add the lemon grass, fish sauce, soy sauce, salt, and sugar and purée again until well combined.

4   Marinate pork for a minimum of 2 hours and up to overnight, making sure marinade is distributed evenly.

5   Remove pork from marinade wiping away excess marinade. Season with kosher salt and freshly ground black pepper.

6   Heat oil in large oven-proof sauté pan. Sear pork chops until golden, being careful not to overcrowd or pork chops will steam instead of caramelize – turn over and place in oven to finish, until internal temperature rises above 140°F.

7   Serve pork over Purée of Roasted Sweet Potato, Pumpkin and Apples and top with a few Pickled Apples. Accompany with Sweet Potato Gratin and Spicy Greens.

SIMPLE STEAK

SERVES 4

At the restaurant we always offer a selection of simple fish and simple steak – extremely simple, but delicious and illustrates the importance of seasoning evenly and generously. This is the ideal dish to mix and match with almost any of the seasonal accompaniments (see pages 131–154).

Four 10–12 ounces New York strip steak
4 tablespoons extra virgin olive oil

Kosher salt, generously to taste
Freshly ground black pepper, generously to taste

1   Preheat grill to medium-high heat or flame.

2   Bring meat to room temperature. This will allow meat to cook most efficiently and evenly and attain the most even and beautiful color. Also, if you choose to cook steak rare it will not be ice cold in center.

3   Drizzle meat with extra virgin olive oil over all sides until glistening.

4   Season generously and evenly with the kosher salt. Always season with salt first, before other spices, so it can penetrate and become integrated into the flavor of the food. Sprinkle seasonings from about 8 inches above the food to get the most even distribution. You will need a little bit more salt than you might think when seasoning in advance of cooking – but instead of a salty layer on the exterior of the meat, as it would be if you seasoned after the meat has been cooked, it will be able to penetrate into the meat and become integrated – bringing out the most flavor of the food. Next, lightly and evenly season with freshly ground pepper – turn and repeat process on other side. The goal is to have every bite taste the same – not to bite into a salty bite, then a bland bite and next a peppery bite.

5   Grill over medium-high to high heat, on either a charcoal or gas grill, placing steaks at a 45 degree angle – lifting and making a quarter turn and then when halfway cooked, flipping steak over midway through cooking and repeating the process of placing at a 45 degree angle and making a quarter turn again to evenly mark steak.

6   Remove and let rest lightly tented in foil for about 6–8 minutes before serving. This will allow the juice in the meat – which creates a lot of the flavor and tenderness – to redistribute and stay within the meat, instead of running out as it would if you cut into the meat right away.

PAN ROASTED PORK CHOPS STUFFED WITH MINCED GULF SHRIMP, MACADAMIA NUTS AND CHÈVRE OVER WILD MUSHROOM CREAM

SERVES 4

To simplify this dish, feel free to serve the stuffing alongside the pork instead of stuffing it.

4 large center cut pork chops
Extra virgin olive oil
Kosher salt, to taste
Freshly ground black pepper
Shrimp Stuffing (recipe follows)

Wild Mushroom Cream (see page 218)
Rough Garlic Mashed Potatoes, one batch
   (see page 152)
Vegetable of the season – a simple preparation such
   as Roasted Farmer's Market Carrots (see page
   143) or Spring Vegetable Mélange (see page 146)
   goes best with this

1   Preheat oven to 425°F.

2   Make deep incision through the center of each
    pork chop and fill with Shrimp Stuffing.

3   Rub Pork chops with extra virgin olive oil until
    glistening and season generously with kosher
    salt and freshly ground black pepper.

4   Heat olive oil over medium-high heat in large,
    oven-proof sauté pan. Sear pork chops, being
    careful not to overcrowd in pan or meat will not
    be able to caramelize properly. Turn over until
    internal temperature rises above 140°F. If exterior
    of chops are beginning to get too dark, place pan
    in oven to finish cooking.

5   To serve, spoon Wild Mushroom Cream onto plate.
    Blot chops briefly on clean towel to absorb any
    excess juice and then place over pool of sauce and
    accompany with Rough Garlic Mashed Potatoes
    and vegetables of the season.

SHRIMP STUFFING

Light cooking oil
1 red bell pepper, finely diced
½ white onion, finely diced
5 large gulf shrimp, diced
½ cup macadamia nuts, chopped coarsely
¾ cup panko Japanese breadcrumbs
Kosher salt, to taste
Freshly ground black pepper

1   Sauté pepper and onion in oil for a few minutes –
    season with kosher salt and freshly ground
    black pepper.

2   Add shrimp and sauté for a few more minutes
    until shrimp just loses translucency.

3   Stir in breadcrumbs and nuts – taste. Adjust
    seasoning and remove from heat.

BEEF TENDERLOIN WITH ACCOUTREMENTS

SERVES 4

This preparation is also great with NY Strip, Delmonico or almost any steak. The flavors and textures are very cozy and fulfilling and ideal in the cold weather.

Four 8 ounces Tournedos of Beef Tenderloin
Kosher salt
Freshly ground black pepper
Extra virgin olive oil
1 cup Stilton, crumbled into large chunks

Caramelized Onions (recipe follows)
Port Macerated Dried Fruit (see page 140),
    may be made up to a week in advance
Rough Garlic Mashed Potatoes, one batch
    (see page 152)
Vegetables of the season such as Sugar Snap Peas with
    Fresh Lime and Mint (see page 141), Chopped and
    Sautéed Brussels Sprouts (see page 135) or Braised
    Fennel with Lemon and Ginger (see page 134)

1 Preheat oven to 425°F.

2 Drizzle tournedos of beef with extra virgin olive oil and rub all over until meat glistens. Season both sides generously with kosher salt and freshly ground black pepper.

3 Heat oven-proof sauté pan over medium-high heat, making sure you have enough room as not to crowd meat or meat will steam instead of being allowed to sear and therefore develop the best texture and flavor as it caramelizes. Shift each piece of meat shortly after placing in pan to ensure it doesn't stick and then allow the meat to cook undisturbed until seared and cooked about halfway (about 4 minutes). Turn tenderloin over and allow to cook until medium rare, about 4 more minutes. If you want to cook more – place in oven for a couple of additional minutes until steak reaches desired level of doneness.

4 Top each tournedo generously with Caramelized Onions and then crumbled Stilton. Transfer pan to oven for a few minutes until Stilton is softened.

5 To serve, place beef in center of each plate and surround with bundles of the accoutrements – Rough Garlic Mashed Potatoes, Port Macerated Fruit and vegetables of the season.

CARAMELIZED ONIONS

2 tablespoons extra virgin olive oil
2 tablespoons salted butter
4 medium Spanish onions, julienned
2 teaspoons kosher salt
1 teaspoon freshly ground pepper

Warm butter and oil over low heat in large shallow pan – add onions and cook stirring frequently until they become deep golden brown – about 25 minutes. Season with kosher salt and freshly ground black pepper. Set aside.

GRILLED MARINATED FLANK WITH MUSTARD CREAM AND DOTTED WITH BALSAMIC REDUCTION

SERVES 4

1½–2 pounds flank
40 cloves of Garlic Marinade (see page 227)
Kosher salt
Freshly ground black pepper
½ cup heavy whipping cream

Mustard Cream (see page 216)
½ recipe Balsamic Reduction, room temperature
   (see page 229)
Rough Garlic Mashed Potatoes, one batch
   (see page 152)
Grilled Pencil-Thin Asparagus (see page 139)

1   Marinate flank, making sure meat is thoroughly surrounded by marinade for minimum of 8 hours and up to 48 hours.

2   Remove flank from marinade and wipe away any excess marinade. Season with Kosher salt and freshly ground black pepper. Grill to medium rare. Let rest 10 minutes lightly tented in foil and then slice as thinly as possible at a deep angle.

3   While flank is resting, warm heavy cream in medium sauce pan and then stir in Mustard Cream – adjust seasoning with kosher salt and freshly ground black pepper.

4   Warm Balsamic Reduction in a separate, small, non-reactive saucepan.

5   To serve, make a pool of Mustard Cream on each plate and using small demitasse spoon dot Mustard Cream with Balsamic Reduction.

6   Fan out steak alongside sauces and serve with Rough Garlic Mashed Potatoes and Grilled Pencil-Thin Asparagus.

Not having a working partner, and never having quite found the right fit for a general manager, I can sometimes feel a little bit stretched thin. At the same time, this situation has almost forced into place my philosophy of the restaurant as a real community where everyone is an integral part of the success and functioning of the restaurant. Unlike what is more common – a restaurant as a transient environment and secondary job – working at eve, not just requests, but demands, a deep level of commitment as a basic starting point. Because of this, each member of the staff gains a certain importance that might not happen otherwise.

There are really no narrow job descriptions at the restaurant and there isn't a lot that is beyond expectation. Everybody at eve really wants the restaurant to be something special and being committed to that same goal, is willing to do whatever that takes. The philosophy that no effort is too great can become contagious and almost a fun challenge – from the waiter who ran into the restaurant from the patio breathless, asking if we had any bones in the house because his customers had their dog with them and wanted to roast the dog a bone – to running to the farmer's market around the corner to get a customer's preferred herb that we didn't have in the kitchen – to making a quick lunch for people who wander in during the day even though we aren't open for lunch. eve will never be a place where the door is locked 5 minutes before closing time as you knock on the window trying to get someone's attention just to be waved away. This might take more effort at times but the feeling it creates, both for us as a group working together and for our customers who are so appreciative, makes it almost invigorating. To me, it is just being thoughtful, but because of the rushed lifestyle we are a part of, just taking the time to be nice sometimes seems a surprise.

We always look for people who are warm, hospitable and genuinely like taking care of people – having a staff with those natural qualities gives us the best chance to achieve that special "je ne sais quoi" that we are always working towards.

SIRLOIN OF LAMB
RUBBED WITH LAVENDER AND WILDFLOWER HONEY

SERVES 4

Four 8 ounce pieces boneless sirloin of lamb *
Lavender and Wildflower Honey Rub (see page 245)
Light olive oil
Kosher salt
Freshly ground black pepper

1 cup Mustard Cream (see page 216)
⅓ cup heavy cream
Gingered Sweet Potato Gratin, one batch
  (see page 151), or Rough Garlic Mashed Potatoes,
  one batch (see page 152)
Vegetables of the Season such as Sugar Snap Peas
  with Fresh Lime and Mint (see page 141) or
  Roasted Farmer's Market Carrots (see page 143)

1   Marinate lamb sirloin in Lavender Wildflower Honey Marinade, making sure lamb is thoroughly surrounded by marinade for minimum of 8 hours and up to 48 hours.

2   Remove lamb from marinade wiping away excess marinade. Season with kosher salt and freshly ground black pepper.

3   Heat olive oil in large oven-proof skillet over medium-high heat – sear lamb – making sure you have enough room not to crowd meat or meat will steam instead of being allowed to sear and therefore develop best texture and flavor as it caramelizes. Shift each piece of meat shortly after placing in pan to ensure it doesn't stick and then allow the meat to cook undisturbed until seared and cooked about halfway (about 4 minutes). Turn steaks over and allow to cook until medium rare, about 4 more minutes. If you want to cook more – place skillet in 400°F oven for a couple of additional minutes until desired level of doneness. Reserve pan for finishing sauce and set lamb aside to rest lightly tented in foil at room temperature. (This lamb is also delicious grilled.)

4   Pour off excess oil from pan and add heavy cream to pan, swirling to incorporate flavor from caramelized bits in saucepan. Stir in Mustard Cream and season to taste with kosher salt and freshly ground black pepper.

5   To serve, blot bottom of lamb with clean towel to remove excess juice. Make pool of Mustard Cream and place lamb overlapping sauce and accompany with Gingered Sweet Potato Gratin and vegetables of the season.

*Available through D'artagnan, see sources, page 248.

CREOLE RATATOUILLE
WITH WARM CAPRIOLE BANON

SERVES 4

This is also delicious with any good goat cheese, Ricotta, Brie, or really any supple, delicious cheese.

1 red onion, fine julienne
1 eggplant, large dice
2 zucchini, large dice
2 yellow squash, large dice
1½ cups crimini mushrooms, quartered
5 fresh thyme springs
10 garlic cloves, smashed
10 ripe tomatoes, medium dice
3 tablespoons sriracha (we use Shark brand)*

¾–1 teaspoon smoked paprika
1¼ teaspoons Chili Mélange (see page 242)
¼ cup Shiraz or other full bodied red wine
1 teaspoon kosher salt or to taste
¼ teaspoon freshly ground black pepper or to taste
1 piece Capriole Banon, broken into 4 equal sized pieces (or other good quality, mild goat cheese)
1 baguette, sliced

1 Preheat oven to 450°F.

2 Roast onion, zucchini, yellow squash, mushrooms and thyme with a little extra virgin olive oil and fairly generous seasoning of kosher salt until just outside begins to blister and inside is just tender. At the restaurant, we roast all vegetables on separate trays which is ideal for preserving the individual taste and cooking evenly and then combine, but roasting all but eggplant together is okay. Roast eggplant on separate tray with the same method.

3 Transfer vegetables to a sauté pan and add garlic and tomatoes. Simmer for 20 minutes allowing them to begin to break down. Add sriracha, smoked paprika, and Spice mixture.

4 Deglaze with wine and simmer until wine is fully incorporated into other ingredients.

5 Adjust generously to taste.

6 Mound warm ratatouille in center of oven-proof plate – top with cheese – place in oven briefly to warm cheese and serve with sliced baguette.

Available at most Asian markets.

One 12-ounce block extra firm tofu, sliced into
    12 pieces, widthwise
Kosher salt
Freshly ground black pepper
Extra virgin olive oil
2 cups Thai BBQ Marinade (see page 227)
1½ cups crushed macadamia nuts, toasted
½ cup chopped tropical dried fruit
1 cup seaweed wakame salad *
½ cup shaved dried coconut

Spicy Roasted Sweet Potatoes, one batch
    (see page 154)
Vegetables of the season such as Spring Vegetable
    Mélange (see page 146) Roasted Farmer's Market
    Carrots (see page 143) or Sugar Snap Peas with
    Fresh Lime and Mint (see page 141)

1 Place Thai BBQ marinade in small, non-reactive
   saucepan and reduce gently over low heat until
   thickened to consistency of peanut butter,
   stirring frequently.

2 Season both sides of tofu generously and evenly
   with kosher salt and freshly ground black pepper.

3 Heat olive oil in large sauté pan and sauté tofu until
   lightly golden, but still tender inside. Remove from
   pan and transfer to an oven proof plate or baking
   sheet lightly greased with olive oil.

4 Brush reduced marinade on tofu slices and place
   under broiler until slightly burnished and bubbly.

5 To assemble, sprinkle tofu with chopped nuts,
   coconut, fruit and wakame – top with second
   layer – repeat two more times using 3 pieces of
   tofu per serving.

6 To serve, place Napoleon in center of each plate –
   surround with vegetable of the season and garnish
   with sliced Spicy Roasted Sweet Potatoes.

*Available at most Asian markets, gourmet grocers
or even grocery store sushi counters.*

FRESH TAGLIATELLE
TOSSED WITH WAKAME AND SUMMER GREENS

SERVES 4

Extra virgin olive oil
¾ cup red onions, fine julienne
¼ cup garlic, minced
1¼ cup good quality, dry white wine
1 teaspoon extra hot sauce (we use Melinda's brand)
4 tablespoons hot sauce (we use Tiger brand)
1 pound fresh tagliatelle, cooked al dente in boiling salted water, tossed lightly in olive oil and set aside at room temperature

2 cups greens, torn – such as baby arugula, Swiss chard, dandelion, beet or mustard greens
1 cup wakame seaweed*
Kosher salt
2 tablespoons extra-virgin olive oil, additional for finishing
Freshly ground black pepper
Black sesame seeds, optional

1   Sauté garlic for about a minute then add red onions and continue to sauté until soft over medium-high heat in a large sauté pan until soft and aromatic – season with kosher salt and freshly ground black pepper. Deglaze with white wine, bring to a simmer and cook for an additional minute or two.

2   Add Melinda's and Tiger Sauce, cooking for an additional minute and add greens, wakame, pasta and then additional extra-virgin olive oil – toss well to combine and adjust seasonings generously.

3   To serve, spoon pasta into large shallow bowls and sprinkle with black sesame seeds.

*Available at most Asian markets, gourmet grocers or even grocery store sushi counters.

PINE NUT ENCRUSTED TALEGGIO WITH BRUSSELS SPROUTS BRAISED IN TOMATO CREAM

SERVES 4

½ cup flour seasoned generously with kosher salt and freshly ground black pepper
Kosher salt
Freshly ground black pepper
4 eggs, lightly beaten with a tablespoon of cream or milk added to create egg wash
2 cups Pine Nut Mixture (recipe follows), in shallow dish

1 pound taleggio, cut into 4
12 Brussels sprouts
1 quart Tomato Cream (see page 223)
Warm, sliced baguette
2 cups baby spinach
¼ cup Parmigiano Reggiano, shredded or shaved

1 Preheat oven to 375°F.

2 Season taleggio with Kosher salt and freshly ground black pepper.

3 Place seasoned flour, egg wash and pine nut mixture – each in a separate, shallow dish.

4 Dredge taleggio in seasoned flour, shaking to remove excess flour, then egg wash, and finally, Pine Nut Mixture, pressing pine nuts firmly onto cheese.

5 Transfer Pine Nut Encrusted Taleggio to refrigerator for a minimum of 15 minutes to set up.

6 Meanwhile, blanch halved Brussels sprouts in boiling salted water for about 3–5 minutes until just fork tender and shock in ice water bath to retain bright green color. When fully cool, dry thoroughly.

7 Finish cooking Brussels sprouts by simmering gently in Tomato Cream until quite soft and tender.

8 Heat olive oil in large oven proof sauté pan and sear taleggio until just golden – transfer to oven until taleggio is soft but still holds its shape.

9 To serve, make a ruffle of baby spinach around perimeter of plate – spoon Tomato Cream and Brussels sprouts into center of plate and sprinkle with Reggiano. Using a flexible spatula lift taleggio gently out of pan and place over Tomato Cream and Brussels sprouts. Accompany with warm sliced baguette.

PINE NUT MIXTURE

2 cups pine nuts
1 cup panko Japanese breadcrumbs
Kosher salt, to taste

Pulse in food processor until combined.

GRILLED EGGPLANT NAPOLEON LAYERED WITH BASIL WALNUT PESTO, FRICASSEE OF WILD MUSHROOMS AND TOMATO CREAM

SERVES 4

1 large eggplant, sliced about ½-inch thick, 12 slices
Extra virgin olive oil
Kosher salt
Freshly ground black pepper
1 quart Tomato Cream (see page 223)

1½ cups Basil Walnut Pesto (see page 231)
2 cups Fricassee of Wild Mushrooms (see page 136)
½ cup herbed goat cheese and boursin, combined equally

1 Preheat oven to 425°F.

2 Sprinkle eggplant slices lightly with kosher salt and let rest about 1 hour.

3 Drizzle both sides of sliced eggplant with extra virgin olive oil, kosher salt and freshly ground black pepper.

4 Sauté eggplant in olive oil in a large oven-proof sauté pan over medium-high heat until golden and tender. Transfer to oven and cook for a few more minutes if eggplant is getting too dark and needs additional cooking.

5 Layer eggplant with spoonful of Tomato Cream, Fricassee of Wild Mushroom, goat cheese and Basil Walnut Pesto. Repeat two more times, using 3 slices of eggplant per serving. Top with additional sauce and cheese.

6 Place Napoleons on greased baking sheet in oven for about 6 minutes until cheese is melted, golden and bubbly.

7 To serve, spoon Tomato Cream onto plate and then place each Napoleon overlapping sauce.

ACCOMPANIMENTS

COOL THAI CUCUMBERS

SERVES 4

1 red onion, thinly julienned
5 small cucumbers, sliced thin at a bias
1 red pepper, thinly julienned
1 cup unseasoned rice wine vinegar (we use
  Marukan brand)
¼ cup plus 1 tablespoon sugar or to taste

1 teaspoon soy sauce (we use Kikkoman brand)
¼ teaspoon crushed red pepper flakes
Kosher salt
Freshly ground black pepper

1 Combine julienned onion, cucumbers and red
   peppers and set aside.

2 In a medium non-reactive pot, combine the sugar
   and the liquid ingredients and simmer for about
   5 minutes, stirring occasionally – until sugar crystals
   have dissolved. Remove from heat and refrigerate
   until cool.

3 When the liquid has cooled completely, add the
   onions, cucumbers, red peppers and crushed red
   pepper. Let stand at least 2 hours before serving.
   Refrigerated, keeps up to 1 week – flavor will
   continue to improve with time.

MARINATED OLIVES

2 cups assorted olives (we use Picholine,
   Nicoise and Arbequina)
⅓ cup extra virgin olive oil
Juice and zest of one lemon
2 tablespoon sherry vinegar
1 teaspoons sriracha (we use Shark brand)*
2 tablespoons Dried Mission Fig and Orange
   Spread with Cognac (see page 211) or
   Adriatic Fig Spread**

⅓ cup sun dried tomatoes, rehydrated and
   cut into fine julienne
4 sprigs fresh thyme
1 bay leaf
Pinch ground ginger

Remove olives from brine and combine all ingredients in non-reactive mixing bowl. Refrigerate overnight before serving – olive will keep refrigerated for several weeks. Store refrigerated, but bring to room temperature before serving.

*Available at most Asian markets.
**Available at Whole Foods or Morgan and York.

SPICY COLESLAW

SERVES 6 – 8

½ cup apple cider vinegar
½ cup sugar
1 tablespoon plus 1 teaspoon kosher salt
¼ teaspoon freshly ground black pepper
1½ cups Traditional Mayonnaise (see page 228)
   or prepared mayonnaise
½ cup extra virgin olive oil
1 tablespoon Dijon mustard

1 tablespoon chili paste (we use Amore brand
   Italian hot chili paste)*
2 tablespoons fresh garlic
1 tablespoon lime juice
1 head white cabbage, shredded
¼ head red cabbage, shredded
1 red onion, fine julienne
1 large carrot, shredded
1 bunch cilantro, rough chop

1 Combine cider vinegar, sugar, kosher salt and black pepper in a medium mixing bowl stirring to combine well. Add mayonnaise, olive oil, mustard, chili paste, garlic and lime juice and stir again to combine well.

2 In a separate, large, mixing bowl combine cabbage, red onion, carrot and cilantro.

3 Pour dressing over vegetables and toss together to incorporate.

4 Adjust seasonings generously to taste.

*Available at most gourmet grocers.

PICKLED LOCAL APPLES

MAKES 1 QUART

We get great apples here in Michigan (which is much appreciated since a good part of the year it is too cold to grow almost anything!), but it is always best to seek out the special ingredients available where you live.

2¼ cups good quality cider vinegar
1½ cups sugar
1 cinnamon stick
2 teaspoons allspice berries

½ teaspoon whole cloves
2 teaspoons fresh ginger, minced
1 quart tart apples, unpeeled and sliced in eighths

1 Combine all ingredients except apples in non-reactive saucepan and warm over medium-low heat, stirring occasionally and bring to a bare simmer.

2 Reduce heat to low and add apples. Bring to a very gentle simmer until apples are just tender – should take about 10 minutes.

3 Allow apples to cool to room temperature and then refrigerate overnight – can be kept refrigerated in an airtight container for several weeks.

BRAISED FENNEL
WITH LEMON AND GINGER

SERVES 4

Light olive oil
2 tablespoons garlic, minced
2 tablespoons ginger, minced
2 fennel bulbs, fine julienne
Kosher salt
Freshly ground black pepper
2 teaspoons Chili Mélange (see page 242)
¼ cup Pernod

3 cups Chicken Essence (see page 68) stock or broth (If using canned chicken broth use College Inn brand.)
Juice from one lemon
½ cup Fresh Herb Butter (see page 33)
1 cup Parmigiano Reggiano, or other good Parmesan

1 Heat oil in large sauté pan and sauté garlic and ginger for several minutes. Add fennel, kosher salt, freshly ground black pepper and Chili Mélange.

2 Deglaze with Pernod and cook for a minute until Pernod is incorporated into fennel.

3 Add Chicken Essence or broth and lemon juice.

4 Reduce at gentle simmer until slightly thickened – about 5 minutes.

5 Add Fresh Herb Butter and Reggiano cheese.

6 Reduce until sauce is slightly thickened and adjust seasoning generously to taste.

CHOPPED AND SAUTÉED BRUSSELS SPROUTS

SERVES 4

4 cups Brussels sprouts, base removed and thinly sliced
1 tablespoon extra virgin olive oil
1 Roma tomato, diced
1½ teaspoons kosher salt, preferably diamond brand

¼ teaspoon freshly ground black pepper
2–3 tablespoons Fresh Herb Butter (see page 33)

1 Prepare ice bath and set aside.

2 Bring pot of salted water to a boil and blanch Brussels sprouts for about 1 minute.

3 Quickly strain Brussels sprouts and place in ice bath to shock.

4 When Brussels sprouts are completely cooled, strain again and dry well on towels.

5 Sauté Brussels sprouts and tomatoes briefly with a small amount of olive oil in large sauté pan over medium-high heat.

6 Add Fresh Herb Butter and stir to combine until just melted but still creamy. Season with kosher salt and freshly ground black pepper and remove quickly from heat.

CREOLE RATATOUILLE

SERVES 4 – 6

1 red onion, fine julienne
1 eggplant, large dice
2 zucchini, large dice
2 yellow squash, large dice
1½ cups crimini mushrooms, quartered
Extra virgin olive oil
Kosher salt, for roasting
5 fresh thyme sprigs

10 garlic cloves, smashed
10 ripe tomatoes, medium dice
3 tablespoons sriracha (we use Shark brand)*
¾–1 teaspoon smoked paprika
1–2 teaspoons Chili Mélange (see page 242)
¼ cup Shiraz or other full bodied red wine
1 teaspoon kosher salt
¼ teaspoon freshly ground black pepper

1 Preheat oven to 450°F.

2 Roast onion, zucchini, yellow squash, mushrooms and thyme with a little extra virgin olive oil and fairly generous seasoning of kosher salt until just outside is nicely browned and beginning to blister and inside is just tender. At the restaurant we roast all vegetables on separate trays that is ideal and then combine, but roasting all but eggplant together is okay. Roast eggplant on separate tray with the same method.

3 Place tomatoes and garlic in a wide non-reactive braising pan and simmer together until garlic begins to soften.

4 Add vegetables, sriracha, smoked paprika, Chili Mélange and Kosher salt and freshly ground black pepper.

5 Deglaze with wine and simmer until wine is fully incorporated with other ingredients and vegetables are tender but retain their form.

6 Adjust seasoning generously to taste.

*Available at most Asian markets.

FRICASSEE OF WILD MUSHROOMS

SERVES 4 – 6

2 pounds assorted cultivated mushrooms, quartered and sliced (domestic, shiitake, portabella, crimini, chanterelle, cèpes)
2½ tablespoons salted butter
3½ tablespoons olive oil
4–5 tablespoons whole shallots, minced
2–2½ tablespoons garlic cloves, minced

3 tablespoons chopped fresh herbs such as flat leaf parsley, chives, chervil, basil, thyme, avoiding cilantro and rosemary as they may overpower flavor of other herbs
1–2 teaspoons kosher salt, to taste
½ teaspoon or more to taste freshly crushed black pepper

1 Brush mushrooms to clean if needed. Trim away tough bottoms of stems (remove stems of shiitake) and slice, quarter or tear into equivalent size pieces.

2 Heat butter and oil in wide, shallow braising pan on medium-low heat – sweat shallots and garlic. Add kosher salt and freshly ground black pepper and sweat for a few additional minutes.

3 Raise heat to medium-high and add mushrooms in batches, shaking pan – mushrooms will exude water and then dry out again. Sauté until tender.

4 Season generously with kosher salt and freshly ground black pepper.

5 Remove from heat and add chopped herbs.

RUSSIAN RIVER MUSHROOMS

SERVES 4

This recipe was adapted by my mother from Helen Brown's West Coast Cookbook. Eating these mushrooms was my favorite treat growing up – my mom only made them once in a while. I don't know why – maybe to keep them so special in our minds.

¼ cup salted butter
½ cup onions, minced
1 pound mushrooms, quartered
1 tablespoon all-purpose flour
½ cup Chicken Essence (see page 68) stock or broth (If using canned broth, use College Inn brand.)

Kosher salt
Freshly ground black pepper, to taste
½ teaspoon crushed dill seed
1 cup sour cream

1 Sauté onions and mushrooms in melted butter in large, wide braising pan until lightly browned.

2 Add flour, stock, salt, pepper, and crushed dill seed.

3 Simmer on low heat, adding sour cream gradually.

4 Adjust seasonings generously to taste.

HARICOTS VERTS
SAUTÉED IN DUCK FAT

SERVES 4

3 cups haricots verts, ends trimmed if needed
3 tablespoons rendered duck fat (preferably pulled
   from cured duck breast prosciutto)*
Kosher salt
Freshly ground black pepper

1   Warm duck fat in large non-stick sauté pan over
    medium-high heat.

2   Add haricots verts and sauté shaking or tossing
    frequently for about 2 minutes at most, until just
    tender – still crisp.

3   Season with kosher salt and freshly ground black
    pepper and eat as soon as possible.

*Available through Durham Tracklements, see sources,
page 248.*

MOROCCAN SPICED CARROTS

SERVES 6 – 8

3 quarts carrots, blanched (see blanching
  instructions below)
½ cup fresh garlic, minced
2 tablespoons Moroccan Spice (see page 239)
2 tablespoons sriracha (we use Shark brand)
1 lemon, juiced

¼ bunch fresh parsley
2 tablespoons brown sugar
Kosher salt, to taste
Freshly ground black pepper, to taste
½ bunch fresh mint, rough chop
1 tablespoon Chili Mélange (see page 242)

1   Blanch carrots in boiling salted water until just tender
    – shock in ice bath and then strain and dry well.

2   Combine carrots with remaining ingredients in large
    mixing bowl.

3   Adjust seasoning generously to taste.

GRILLED PENCIL-THIN ASPARAGUS

SERVES 4

Good asparagus starts becoming available in March and my favorite is the tender, pencil-thin asparagus that takes only a minute or two to cook. There are only a few ingredients in this recipe but it is surprisingly flavorful and goes with just about anything.

1 large bunch asparagus, about 1 pound
   stalky ends removed – if any
Extra virgin olive oil
Kosher salt
Freshly ground black pepper

1 Heat charcoal or gas grill to medium-high to high heat.

2 In large mixing bowl, drizzle asparagus with extra virgin olive oil and season generously with kosher salt and freshly ground black pepper and toss together. Asparagus should be moist and glistening, but not oily.

3 Just before grilling, drizzle asparagus with a little additional extra virgin olive oil.

4 Line up asparagus in single layer running opposite direction as grates of the grill so they don't fall through.

5 As soon as asparagus begins to blister, push asparagus with tongs to roll and allow to blister slightly around perimeter.

6 Remove as soon as asparagus is barely cooked – should be just barely tender inside. The whole process will only take a couple of minutes depending on the thickness of your asparagus.

7 Taste and adjust seasonings – if too salty, drizzle asparagus with a bit more olive oil.

SPICY GREENS

SERVES 4

Even though this dish has bold flavor, it is very versatile and is a great complement to anything from grilled meat or fish to omelets, grilled pizzas, quesadillas and almost everything else we've experimented with.

2 tablespoons light olive oil
1 cup red onions, fine dice
2 teaspoons jalapeño, minced
1 tablespoon plus 1 teaspoon garlic, minced
Kosher salt
Freshly ground black pepper, to taste

1 quart kale, torn
1 quart Swiss chard, torn
2 tablespoons sriracha (we use Shark brand)*
2 tablespoons Chicken Essence (see page 68) stock or broth (If using canned chicken broth, use College Inn brand.)

1 Heat oil in large sauté pan over medium-high heat and sauté red onions and jalapeños until they begin to soften, about 5 minutes.

2 Add garlic and continue to sauté until fragrant and soft. Season with kosher salt and freshly ground black pepper.

3 Add greens beginning with kale, and after a few minutes add chard and sauté until leaves begin to wilt.

4 Add 1 tablespoon sriracha and then Chicken Essence or broth and allow greens to steam briefly in liquid.

5 When most of the liquid is absorbed, add remaining tablespoon sriracha – adjust seasonings generously to taste.

Available at most Asian markets.

PORT MACERATED DRIED FRUIT

MAKES 1 QUART

1 cup dried apricots, whole if small, halved at an angle if large
1 cup dried dates, halved

1 cup small prunes, whole
1 cup figs, halved lengthwise
2 cups Ruby Port

1 Bring port to a boil, then reduce to simmer until port thickens slightly – about 5 minutes.

2 Add fruit, stir well to combine and remove from heat. Can be kept refrigerated in an airtight container for several weeks.

SPIKED APPLESAUCE

SERVES 4 – 6

6 Granny Smith apples, unpeeled and sliced in eighths
¼ stick salted butter
⅓ cup Brown Sugar Spice (see page 242)
1½ teaspoons cinnamon
¼ teaspoon cloves
¼ teaspoon allspice

¼ teaspoon nutmeg
2 pieces star anise
Pinch of kosher salt
½ cup apple juice
6 cups hard cider
3 cups dark rum

1 Place apples, butter, and Brown Sugar Spice and spices in large non-reactive saucepan and sauté over medium heat until apples begin to soften, about 10 minutes.

2 Add apple juice, hard cider and rum and continue cooking until soft, about 20 minutes, stirring occasionally and mashing lightly with the back of a spoon.

SUGAR SNAP PEAS
WITH FRESH LIME AND MINT

SERVES 4 – 6

4 cups sugar snap peas
1 tablespoon extra virgin olive oil
Kosher salt
Freshly ground black pepper

1 teaspoon freshly squeezed lime juice
2 tablespoons fresh mint, chiffonade, (ribbon cut)
2 teaspoons Fresh Herb Butter (see page 33)

1 Heat olive oil over medium-high heat in a large sauté pan and sauté sugar snap peas quickly – about 2 minutes – should still be crisp and bright green. Season generously with kosher salt and freshly ground black pepper.

2 Remove from heat and add lime juice, mint and Fresh Herb Butter tossing to combine well.

3 Adjust seasonings generously to taste and eat as soon as possible.

ROASTED FARMER'S MARKET CARROTS

SERVES 4

2 bunches thin, tender carrots, most of stem removed – leaving about 2-inches, rinsed, scrubbed and dried (about 1 pound)

Extra virgin olive oil
Kosher salt
Freshly ground black pepper

1 Preheat oven to 450°F.

2 In large mixing bowl, drizzle carrots with extra virgin olive oil and season generously with kosher salt and freshly ground black pepper and toss together. Carrots should be moist and glistening, but not oily.

3 Place on sheet tray and drizzle again with extra virgin olive oil.

4 Roast in oven – shaking pan occasionally – until carrots begin to caramelize and blister – they should still hold their shape – time varies with size of carrots, about 15–20 minutes.

COOL MARINATED BROCCOLI

SERVES 4 – 6

This is the traditional broccoli salad I grew up with – it is the all-American version of the combination of sweet, spicy and savory flavors that I love together.

¾ pound mushrooms, sliced
1 bunch broccoli florets and stems, cut at long bias (about 8 cups)
1 bunch green onions, sliced at long bias

¼ red onion, fine julienne
Simple Vinaigrette (recipe follows)

1 Toss dressing with vegetables – combining well. Pour dressing over vegetables – reserving some dressing for the next day to refresh salad for leftovers.

2 Adjust seasoning generously to taste.

SIMPLE VINAIGRETTE

¾ cup sugar
2 teaspoons kosher salt
2 teaspoons paprika
½ cup plus 1 tablespoon red wine vinegar
2 teaspoons celery seed
2 tablespoons onion powder
½ cup light olive oil
½ cup extra virgin olive oil
Pinch of crushed red pepper flakes, or to taste
1 teaspoon freshly squeezed orange juice

Combine all ingredients and let stand for several hours before serving.

1 pound dry orzo, cooked al dente in boiling, salted water, strained and drizzled with olive oil

Light olive oil, for cooking

3–4 tablespoons extra virgin olive oil

4 cups shiitake mushrooms, stems removed, fine julienne

2 tablespoons garlic, minced

2¼ teaspoons kosher salt

¼–½ teaspoon freshly ground black pepper

1 tablespoon plus 1 teaspoon Chili Mélange (see page 242)

1 tablespoon Chinese five spice

½ cup Fresh Herb Butter, just melted, but still creamy (see page 33)

1 bunch scallions, sliced at long, thin bias

1–2 tablespoons extra virgin olive oil, for finishing orzo

1 Place warm orzo in large mixing bowl.

2 Heat oil in large sauté pan and begin sautéing mushrooms over high heat for about 2 minutes.

3 Reduce heat to medium and add garlic, kosher salt, freshly ground black pepper and five spice.

4 Add cooked orzo and toss to re-warm.

5 Remove from heat and transfer to mixing bowl. Toss with melted Fresh Herb Butter, olive oil and scallions – toss well to incorporate – taste and adjust seasonings generously. Best to over-season slightly as orzo can act as a sponge and flavor will dissipate quickly.

6 This dish tastes best served at warm room temperature.

SLOW COOKED BLACK BEANS

2 tablespoons garlic, minced
½ medium onion, rough chop
¼ yellow bell pepper, rough chop
¼ green bell pepper, rough chop
¼ red bell pepper, rough chop
½ jalapeño or other chili pepper, seeded and minced
¾ pound bacon, medium dice
¾ cup Roma tomatoes, medium dice
4 cups cooked black beans (If using cans, use El Ebro brand.)

2 heaping tablespoons canned puréed chipotle peppers (puréed with sauce)
1 tablespoon sriracha, (we use Shark brand)*
2 bay leaves
½ teaspoon cumin
1 teaspoon dried Mexican oregano
1–2 teaspoons kosher salt or to taste
Pinch of freshly ground black pepper
¼ teaspoon red wine vinegar
Pinch of sugar or to taste

1 In food processor, purée garlic, onions, bell peppers and jalapeños.

2 Cook bacon in wide shallow braising pan over medium heat and render fat. Discard bacon, but retain bacon fat in pan.

3 Place ingredients from food processor into pan with hot fat and sauté over medium heat, stirring frequently until liquid has evaporated.

4 Add tomatoes and sauté about 5 minutes.

5 Add beans, chipotle peppers, sriracha, bay leaves, cumin, oregano, kosher salt and freshly group black pepper and simmer gently until thickened – about 20–30 minutes.

6 Remove from heat and add red wine vinegar and sugar to taste.

7 Adjust seasoning generously to taste and remove bay leaves before serving.

*Available at most Asian markets.

BULGUR WHEAT

SERVES 4 – 6

1 cup bulgur wheat, uncooked
Kosher salt, for cooking bulgur
1 cup pine nuts, toasted
1 cup dried apricots, minced
¼ bunch parsley, rough chop
½ bunch mint, rough chop
¼–½ cup light olive oil
2 teaspoons Moroccan Spice (see page 239)

2 teaspoons Chili Mélange (see page 242)
2 teaspoons sherry vinegar, to taste
1 teaspoons sriracha (we use Shark brand)*
1–2 tablespoons packed brown sugar
½–1 teaspoons kosher salt
Freshly ground black pepper

1 Cook bulgur by bringing 2 cups of salted cold water to a boil in a medium saucepan.

2 Add bulgur as soon as water comes to a boil – cover tightly and then remove from heat immediately. Let rest for half an hour undisturbed. Transfer to large mixing bowl, fluff and then allow to come to room temperature.

3 Add remaining ingredients gently and adjust seasoning generously to taste.

*Available at most Asian markets.

SPRING VEGETABLE MÉLANGE

SERVES 6 – 8

Light olive oil
1 medium carrot, cut at a long bias about ¼-inch thick
1 red, yellow or orange bell pepper, cut into wedges
1 small zucchini, cut at a long bias about ¼-inch thick
1 small summer squash, cut at a long bias about ¼-inch thick
Kosher salt
Freshly ground black pepper

½ red onion, cut into wedges
1 cup ramps, cleaned and any dry or slimy ends removed, cut in half lengthwise
¾ cup sugar snap peas
1 cup fiddlehead ferns
¾ cup grape tomatoes, halved
3 tablespoons Fresh Herb Butter (optional) (see page 33)

1 Heat olive oil in a large sauté pan over medium-high heat and begin by sautéing the carrots and ramps – sauté for several minutes and then add remaining vegetables with the exception of sugar snap peas and tomatoes – season generously with kosher salt and freshly ground black pepper.

2 Add sugar snap peas and fiddlehead ferns and continue to sauté for a few more minutes until vegetables are just beginning to soften but are still crisp inside then add tomatoes and toss just to incorporate.

3 Add Fresh Herb Butter, if desired, tossing with vegetables – butter should just melt, but remain creamy. Taste and add kosher salt and freshly ground black pepper generously to taste.

COCONUT GINGER RICE

SERVES 4

This recipe is adapted from Steve Raichlen's Miami Spice cookbook. Ours is a bit more full-flavored and pungent from additional garlic and ginger – but still delicate enough to be a versatile accompaniment.

1 tablespoon light olive oil
1 tablespoon salted butter
1 tablespoon minced fresh garlic
2 tablespoons minced fresh ginger
1 cup long grain white rice
1 cup Coconut Milk (see page 231) or use Chakaoh brand

1¼ cups Chicken Essence (see page 68), stock or broth (If using canned broth, use College Inn brand.)
1 teaspoon kosher salt
Freshly ground black pepper, generously to taste

1   Preheat oven to 350ºF

2   Heat oil and butter in heavy pan on medium heat. Add garlic and ginger and sweat until white, puffy and aromatic. Add rice and sauté until grains of rice are shiny.

3   Add coconut milk, Chicken Essence and kosher salt to taste – stir once gently and bring to a boil. Reduce to a simmer, cover pan, place in preheated oven and cook rice until liquid is absorbed – about 30 minutes. When adding salt, you should actually be able to taste salt or there will not be enough to penetrate into the rice. It is always better to add salt to a starchy ingredient like rice or pasta before cooking so it can integrate into the ingredient during the cooking process, bringing out the best flavor.

4   Remove pan from heat and let rice stand, covered and undisturbed for 15 minutes. Taste small amount to determine if needs additional salt and pepper. If additional seasoning is needed, sprinkle evenly over surface of rice and then fluff gently to incorporate.

BETO'S GRATIN

Every night, just before service, from October through March, we make our Gingered Sweet Potato Gratin. It is one of those dishes that is always delicious, but can vary slightly depending on anything from the subtle differences in the condition of the ingredients to who is preparing it. Every night when I taste the gratin I can tell immediately who in the kitchen made it (even though we were all supposedly following the same recipe).

Well, when we started the recipe testing for this book we really started focusing on the gratin. If it came out especially good I would corner the person who made it – interrogate them, asking "did you make the gratin? Do you remember exactly what you did? EXACTLY?" I would ask them to make it again and write down everything they did to the pinch of salt – every slight variation. They would make it again and it would come out terrible – worse than it had ever been – I would make it myself, painstaking, for a person who generally cooks by eye and by taste, writing down every drop of cream added, subtracting every spoonful of cream removed when tasting – and it seemed like it didn't even resemble the same dish I had originally created. Maybe we were over-thinking it, concentrating too hard.

One night the fate fell on Roberto (or Bobby or Beto – he has numerous nicknames as the restaurant "favorite" since the day he started as a dishwasher). Beto eventually became a prep cook and is now cooking on the line. He always does a great job and has a great natural palate. Unfortunately for him, he had made an absolutely delicious gratin and didn't know what he was in for. I asked him the same series of questions – "did he make the gratin, could he replicate it?" He answered me very seriously "yes Eva, I know what I did, yes, I can do it again" – No flavor – worst gratin yet. He made another batch to bake while he did the nightly cleaning – it still wasn't quite right. At 2 o'clock in the morning, after dinner service was over and the kitchen was clean, he came to me asking to make it again. Obsessed, he came in the next day on Sunday, his day off, to make it again. I can't say that his version of the original recipe was the one that made it into the book (but mine wasn't either). It was weeks later that we finally got the recipe down on paper – The Elusive Gratin – it was down to the wire. Throughout the recipe testing process everybody that tasted the gratin from outside the kitchen always loved it, but in the kitchen, we were obsessed – we knew what it should be.

GINGERED SWEET POTATO GRATIN

SERVES 4

If you have any leftovers of this dish, make sure to try out the Sweet Potato Cream AKA Sweet Potato Gratin Soup.

10 ounces Yukon Gold potatoes
6 ounces sweet potatoes
2 whole garlic cloves, split lengthwise
1¼ cups Gruyère, shredded
1¼ cups smoked mozzarella, shredded (reserve ½ cup for finishing gratin)
1½ cups heavy whipping cream
1 tablespoon fresh ginger, minced
1 tablespoon fresh garlic, minced
1 tablespoon onion, minced

¼ cup Caramelized Onions (recipe follows)
¼ heaping teaspoon ground fresh nutmeg
2 teaspoons kosher salt
¼ teaspoon freshly ground black pepper
¼ teaspoon white pepper
¼ teaspoon cayenne pepper, or more to taste
Butter, for greasing pan
Split garlic cloves, for rubbing pans

1 Preheat oven to 350°F.

2 Butter large casserole pan and rub with cut side of split garlic cloves (1½ quart Le Creuset pans are ideal for this).

3 Combine all ingredients except potatoes and additional ½ cup reserved cheese.

4 Slice potatoes as thin as possible – about ⅛ inch thickness and add to cream mixture.

5 Transfer to buttered casserole dish and sprinkle with remaining ½ cup cheese.

6 Bake until golden on top and potatoes are tender (about 1 hour).

CARAMELIZED ONIONS

2 teaspoons extra virgin olive oil
2 teaspoons salted butter
1 medium Spanish onion, fine julienne
Kosher salt
Freshly ground black pepper

Warm butter and oil over low heat in large shallow pan – add onions and cook stirring frequently until they become deep golden brown – about 25 minutes. Season with kosher salt and freshly ground black pepper. Set aside.

POTATO LATKES

SERVES 4 – 6

6 Idaho Russet potatoes
5 onions, finely grated resting in their liquid
1 cup matzoh meal, unsalted
½ cup salted butter, melted
3 eggs

1½ tablespoons Kosher salt
½ teaspoon freshly ground black pepper
Additional salted butter and light cooking oil

1   Gently lift grated onions out of their liquid (do not squeeze) and place in large mixing bowl.

2   Grate potatoes and squeeze gently to get rid of excess liquid before adding to grated onions. Add potatoes to onions as you grate, so potatoes do not discolor.

3   Add matzoh meal, melted butter, eggs and salt and pepper immediately after combining potatoes and onions.

4   Heat oil and then butter in sauté pan and fry latkes until deep golden and just set. Flip and sprinkle lightly with kosher salt. Continue cooking until second side is crisp and golden and potatoes are cooked through. Remove to plate lined with paper towel to absorb excess oil and eat as soon as possible.

ROUGH GARLIC MASHED POTATOES

SERVES 4 – 6

1½ pounds Yukon Gold potatoes
5 garlic cloves, whole
2 tablespoons garlic, minced
¼ cup light olive oil
¾ cup heavy whipping cream, at room temperature
3 tablespoons salted butter, cubed and cold

1½ tablespoons kosher salt
½ teaspoon freshly ground black pepper

1   Preheat over to 375°F.

2   Place potatoes and whole garlic cloves in a medium pot, cover with cold water and bring to a boil. When water comes to a boil, add salt and continue cooking potatoes until they are fork tender.

3   While potatoes are cooking, heat oil to medium-high in small saucepan and add minced garlic. Remove from heat immediately. Garlic should puff up and become fragrant and white. Strain garlic and keep oil for another use.

4   Strain potatoes well – transfer to sheet tray and place in oven for 5 minutes to dry out.

5   Place potatoes in large bowl. Sprinkle minced garlic, kosher salt and freshly ground black pepper evenly over surface. Incorporate butter and cream gradually adding alternatively while mashing with a hand potato masher. As you continue to mash, be careful not to overwork the potatoes or they will bind up and become tight.

6   Adjust seasoning generously to taste adding butter and cream as you desire – should be light, moist and very flavorful.

I think almost everything tastes better cooked in duck fat. When a well known restaurateur came to visit our little kitchen, he was shocked to see a portable deep fryer full of duck fat. The best duck fat in the world, however, comes from the back of TR Durham's duck breast prosciutto – it develops an incredible taste during the curing process and will probably inspire you to come up with even more things to cook in it.

⅓ cup duck fat, rendered (preferably pulled from cured duck breast proscuitto)*
1 pound fingerling potatoes, sliced thin lengthwise
½ Spanish onion, julienned

Kosher salt to taste
Freshly ground black pepper
Chili Mélange (see page 242), to taste

1   Heat duck fat over medium heat in a large non-stick or carbon steel sauté pan. Add potatoes and begin to sauté until potatoes start to become tender and turn golden – they will be about halfway cooked.

2   Add onions and then season very generously with kosher salt, freshly ground black pepper and Chili Mélange and continue to sauté, shaking the pan often and adjusting the heat as needed until potatoes are crisped and golden outside and tender inside. Taste and adjust seasoning generously.

Available through Durham Tracklements, see sources, page 248.

SPICY ROASTED SWEET POTATOES

SERVES 4

Like the Simple Fish and Simple Steak, making this dish is a great way to practice the art of seasoning.

2 sweet potatoes, unpeeled and sliced ¼-inch thick
Extra virgin olive oil
Kosher salt

Freshly ground black pepper
Chili Mélange (see page 242)

1   Preheat oven to 475°F.

2   In large mixing bowl, drizzle potatoes with extra virgin olive oil and toss together until lightly coated (just glistening).

3   Lay sweet potatoes side by side on sheet tray, being careful not to overcrowd. Sprinkle evenly and generously with kosher salt, and lightly with freshly ground black pepper and Chili Mélange, in that order. Flip them over and repeat procedure on other side. It is always best to season with salt first so it can penetrate and become integrated with the flavor of the main ingredient.

4   Drizzle lightly with some additional extra virgin olive oil and roast, until golden and blistered, shaking pan occasionally while cooking. This should take about 20 minutes. While somewhat labor-intensive, it is best to remove sweet potatoes one-by-one as they finish, as potatoes nearest the edge will finish before those in the center of the pan.

DESSERTS

LEMON SOUR CREAM CAKE

MAKES TWO 9-INCH CAKES, SEVEN 4½-INCH CAKES OR 24 LARGE MUFFINS

Because this is the only cake I can make, we make it in all shapes and sizes at the restaurant. We make it for weddings, we make it for birthdays and miniature ones for the dessert menu. Luckily, everyone always goes crazy over it and so I don't have to build up my baking repertoire. Most of our desserts, while sweeter than savory, are more like cooking than baking – custards, crisps, crumbles and other things that have a less scientific, and more forgiving nature.

3 cups sifted all-purpose flour
¼ teaspoon baking soda
½ teaspoon salt
½ pound salted butter
2 teaspoons vanilla extract
3 cups sugar
6 eggs

1 cup sour cream
Zest of one lemon
2½ tablespoons lemon juice
Ripe seasonal fruit, sliced
Lemon Curd (see page 169)
Brown Sugar Cream (see page 161)

1 Preheat oven to 350°F.

2 Butter and flour cake pans.

3 Sift together flour, baking soda, and salt and set aside.

4 In a large bowl in an electric mixer, cream the butter. Add vanilla and gradually add the sugar. Beat until fluffy.

5 Add eggs, two at a time, beating until thoroughly incorporated after each addition, and for a couple of minutes after last addition, scraping the bowl with a rubber spatula as necessary to keep the ingredients well mixed.

6 On the lowest speed add half of the dry ingredients, then all of the sour cream and lemon juice and zest, and then the balance of the dry ingredients, scraping the bowl with the spatula and beating only until smooth after each addition – be extremely careful not to over-mix or cake will bind up and become tight.

7 Pour into pan. Level top by rotating pan briskly back and forth several times. Bake about 1 hour for 8-inch cake, about 30–45 minutes for 4½-inch cake and about 20–30 minutes for 1 cup muffins – or until cake springs back slightly upon touch.

8 Cool cake in pan for about 15 minutes – and then remove by running thin knife around edge of pan pressing into pan and then covering with rack – inverting cake – removing pan and covering other side with rack to invert again.

9 Let cool to room temperature and garnish with sliced fruit, Lemon Curd and Brown Sugar Cream.

CUP OF CHOCOLATE

SERVES 6

Both the white and dark cups of chocolate are pretty decadent – a demitasse with a dollop of brown sugar cream is usually the perfect amount and way to finish a meal. We have found a couple of amazing wine pairings for these – the white pairs astonishingly well with a Pedro Ximenez Sherry and the dark with a Banyuls.

3 cups heavy whipping cream
1 cup half and half
1 pound Callebaut Semi Sweet Chocolate, or your favorite
¼ pound Cuizel 72% dark chocolate, or your favorite
¼ pound El Ray 41% milk chocolate, or your favorite

2 teaspoons vanilla
1 egg yolk
1 cup Brown Sugar Cream (see page 161)

1 Heat the cream and half and half in a medium, heavy duty saucepan.

2 Reduce heat to low and whisk in chocolate.

3 Temper egg yolk by adding a small amount of the chocolate mixture into egg yolk – stirring to combine and then slowly adding egg yolk mixture back into chocolate.

4 Add vanilla.

5 Pour into demitasse cups and top with a spoonful of Brown Sugar Cream.

CUP OF WHITE CHOCOLATE

SERVES 6

2 cups heavy cream
2 cups white chocolate
1 egg yolk
1 teaspoon vanilla
1 tablespoon Makers Mark

Brown Sugar Cream (recipe below)

1 Heat the cream in medium, heavy bottomed saucepan.

2 Reduce heat to low and whisk in chocolate.

3 Temper egg yolk by adding a small amount of the white chocolate mixture into egg yolk – stirring to combine and then slowly adding egg yolk mixture back into white chocolate.

4 Add vanilla.

5 Finish with Makers Mark and remove from heat.

6 Pour into demitasse cups and top with a spoonful of Brown Sugar Cream.

BROWN SUGAR CREAM

MAKES 4 CUPS

1 pint heavy whipping cream
¼ cup brown sugar
2 teaspoons vanilla
2 tablespoons sour cream

1 Whip cream with whisk in mixing bowl or electric mixer until slightly thickened.

2 Add brown sugar, continuing to whip. When stiff peaks form, add vanilla and sour cream.

SUMMERTIME SUNDAE

SERVES 4

Good quality vanilla ice cream
Raspberry Purée (recipe follows)
1½ cups Lemon Curd (see page 169)

Brown Sugar Cream (see page 161)
1 heaping cup ripe summer berries – blueberries, blackberries, raspberries

1 Scoop ice cream into dish.

2 Drizzle with Raspberry Purée.

3 Top with Lemon Curd, Brown Sugar Cream and ripe summer berries and eat as soon as possible.

RASPBERRY PURÉE

2½ cups raspberries
¼ cup sugar

1 In blender or food processor purée raspberries with sugar.

2 Strain and warm in non-reactive saucepan over medium low heat until sugar crystals dissolve.

3 Cool to room temperature.

CARAMEL-RUM CREAM

MAKES ABOUT 2 CUPS

1 pound light brown sugar
1½ sticks unsalted butter, cold
¼ cup dark rum

1 cup heavy whipping cream
1 tablespoon freshly squeezed orange juice

1 Combine sugar and butter (cut in pieces) in saucepan over medium heat, stirring until well combined and sugar is almost dissolved.

2 Add rum and cook for 5 minutes.

3 Add cream and cook for 5 more minutes.

4 Remove from heat and add freshly squeezed orange juice.

APPLE, PEAR AND SUN DRIED CHERRY CRUMBLE

SERVES 6 – 8

FRUIT MIXTURE

1 cup sugar
½ cup all-purpose flour
½ teaspoon cinnamon
½ teaspoon nutmeg
2 Granny Smith apples, sliced into eighths
1 just-ripe pear, sliced into eighths
½ cup sun dried cherries

CRUMBLE MIXTURE

2 sticks salted butter
¾ cup brown sugar, firmly packed
2 cups flour

Vanilla ice cream
Maple Cream (recipe below)

---

1   Preheat oven to 350°F.

2   Lightly butter large casserole dish (2 quart Le Creuset Casserole is ideal).

3   Combine sugar, flour, cinnamon and nutmeg in mixing bowl and set aside.

4   Combine fruit and place into buttered casserole dish.

5   Sprinkle dry ingredients mixture over fruit quickly to prevent fruit from browning and toss to combine.

6   In a medium saucepan, melt butter, remove from heat, and add brown sugar and flour simultaneously – stir gently to combine and then break into large clumps, not crumbs.

7   Crumble clumps over fruit.

8   Bake for about an hour or until crumble is golden brown and fruit is tender.

7   To serve, spoon generous portion of crumble onto center of a shallow bowl. Top with scoop of vanilla ice cream. Drizzle Maple Cream on and around crumble at table just before eating.

MAPLE CREAM

It's pretty hard to go wrong with pure maple syrup, but we prefer the rich and rustic flavor of grade B amber as opposed to the more refined and elegant grade A.

Makes 1½ cups

1 cup heavy whipping cream
½ cup Vermont grade B amber maple syrup

Combine ingredients.

POLENTA BISCUITS
WITH CASHEL BLUE CHEESE

SERVES 6

2 cups berries or other ripe fruit of the season
2 tablespoons wildflower honey*
1 teaspoon fresh lime juice
½ pound Cashel blue cheese or favorite good
   quality blue cheese

¾ cup Damson Plum, Dried Apricot Jam with
   Crystallized Ginger (see jams pages 202–213)
   or favorite jam
6 Polenta Biscuits (recipe follows)

1 Gently toss berries with honey and lime juice in
   non-reactive mixing bowl – set aside for about
   15 minutes.

2 Place crumbled Cashel blue cheese over biscuits
   pressing gently into top of biscuit and place biscuits
   back into 350°F oven until cheese softens.

3 To serve, place biscuit in center of plate – top with
   a teaspoonful of jam and spoon berries onto plate
   around biscuit.

BISCUITS

½ cup plus 2 tablespoons finely ground cornmeal**
½ cup plus 2 tablespoons flour
3 tablespoons plus 1 teaspoon sugar
1½ teaspoons baking powder
1 teaspoon salt
1 egg
¾ cup plus 1 tablespoon half and half
⅔ stick salted butter, melted, cooled to room
   temperature

1 Preheat oven to 350°F.

2 Lightly grease 6 of the 12 cups of a large 1 cup
   measure muffin tin.

3 Combine dry ingredients in a large bowl and
   make a well in the center.

4 Combine liquid ingredients in a separate
   mixing bowl.

5 Pour liquids into well, and stir until barely combined.

6 Spoon batter into muffin tins and bake until just set
   and golden – about 15 to 20 minutes. Keep oven on
   for finishing the dish. Let the muffins cool slightly for
   about 5 minutes and then remove to a sheet tray for
   finishing the dish.

*Available at Cohoctah Honey Works, see sources,
page 248.
**Available through Zingerman's Deli, see sources,

KENNY AND THE ICE CREAM INVENTORY

Ken Harrington Colón holds the record for the most interviews ever given to one person at eve – The Restaurant. When I first interviewed Kenny, I didn't really know what to make of him – he had this huge smile and seemed so positive and optimistic that it was hard to know if it could possibly be genuine. Kenny was working at the University Of Michigan snack bar, which was his only food-related work experience, but had been promoted to manager – a position that had been created for him because of his ingenuity. He had grown up in Puerto Rico, Thailand and Mexico, seemed really into food and very eager to learn how to cook. I asked him to come back for a second interview to get to know him a little bit better, but I still wasn't quite sure what to make of him. This kept going on – periodically he would call to check on the status of his application, and I would ask him back for another interview. I am generally pretty decisive and feel I have good intuition, especially with interviews, but I just didn't quite know what to make of Kenny. He was always equally enthusiastic and would come back as cheerful as ever, with his huge smile as if this was totally normal procedure. After seven interviews, I decided to give it a try and finally hired Kenny.

When he came in with the rest of our opening staff for his first day I got him set up at a prep table and showed him how to clean scallops. A few minutes later, I returned to the kitchen to see Kenny propped up at his work station, sitting on a brand new designer bar stool he had taken upon himself to bring in from the dining room. I was pretty surprised and explained to him that I knew he didn't have a lot of formal restaurant experience, but sitting while you work was not kitchen protocol as it didn't help maintain one's energy and focus. It was the week before the restaurant opened and there was a lot going on so I knew I basically needed to think of something constructive for Kenny to do to keep him occupied. I asked him to go next door, where our freezers were, and do a thorough inventory of our ice creams.

At the time we were getting beautiful Indian style Kulfis that we had to pick up by driving to Windsor at the Canadian border, bring through customs and rush back on dry ice to the restaurant. Because of this, it was vital that we get an accurate inventory in order to schedule these ice cream trips. Kenny went off to the basement next door to do the inventory. A half hour went by and I noticed that Kenny wasn't back – another half an hour, and still no Kenny. I was about to pull myself away from everything going on in the kitchen and go look for him when he came back, smiling and proudly holding out a piece of paper. On it was a very precise drawing, with each tub of ice cream hand-drawn to size and neatly labeled, showing exact levels of each ice cream – like a topographical map – including the slightest indentations where each scoop had been removed.

Ice Cream Levels as of 9-14

Rum Raisin   coconut   mango   pistachio

Rum
Raisin

Even more than professional or educational experience, I have always looked for people who were just nice, intelligent, interesting, have a great work ethic, love to learn and love to eat. Sometimes this demands a little more patience, but I think it is worth it for the overall feeling it brings to the restaurant. Kenny ended up working very successfully in almost every area of the restaurant. He remained just as optimistic and positive as he was at his first interview, but it was genuine and he was a very good person to have in the hectic, and sometimes stressful, environment of a restaurant. Somehow, the more stressful the situation, the bigger his smile got. But – we will still never let Kenny live down his first day at the restaurant.

AUTUMN SPICED FLAN

SERVES 6

½ cup sugar
3 tablespoons water

1 tablespoon ground ginger
¼ teaspoon nutmeg
¼ teaspoon cloves
½ teaspoon ground cinnamon

¼ cup crystallized ginger, minced
½ cup sweetened condensed milk
1 cup cream
1½ teaspoons vanilla extract

4 eggs

TO MAKE THE CARAMEL

1 Preheat oven to 350ºF.

2 Heat together water and sugar over medium flame until it is caramelized and deep golden brown, about 10 minutes. Make sure the mixture doesn't burn.

3 Pour equal amounts into 6 custard cups to evenly coat the bottom of each cup.

TO MAKE THE CUSTARD

1 Combine all custard ingredients, except eggs and pour into a non-reactive pan. Simmer slowly for 15 minutes to combine the flavors.

2 Crack the eggs and beat together. Temper eggs by slowly pouring some of the cream mixture into the eggs and then adding egg mixture back into cream mixture.

3 Pour the custard mixture into the cups and line up in 2-inch deep baking pan. Add about 1-inch of hot water to pan to create a water bath and cook until just set – about 45 minutes. Remove custard from oven and allow to cool in the refrigerator for 6 hours. The flan is then ready to be flipped gently, and served – crystallized ginger should float at the surface intermingled with caramel. (If difficult to remove – warm bottom of dish in hot water briefly to help release.)

LEMON CURD

MAKES ABOUT 2 QUARTS

This recipe makes quite a bit, but keeps well for up to a month refrigerated and is really nice to have on hand – serve it over ice cream, with biscuits or with a bowl of fresh fruit.

10 lemons (juice and zest)
3 sticks unsalted butter

4½ cups sugar
8 eggs, well beaten

1   In double boiler, melt butter.

2   Add lemon juice, zest and sugar and stir until sugar
    crystals are dissolved.

3   Add beaten eggs and stir frequently until ribbon
    forms when stirred and mixture coats the back
    of a spoon.

FIG FRITTERS
WITH HONEYED YOGURT

SERVES 4

1 cup Greek sheep's milk yogurt*
¼ cup wildflower honey**
¼ cup sugar
1 teaspoon cinnamon
8 wonton squares

1 cup Port Macerated Dried Fruit (see page 140)
Light cooking oil, for frying
2 tablespoons wildflower honey for garnish

1   Combine yogurt and honey and set aside.

2   Combine sugar and cinnamon and set aside.

3   Place a spoonful of fruit in center of each wonton. Brush edges of wonton with water and fold corner to opposite side creating triangle.

4   Deep fry at 350°F in light cooking oil until golden.

5   To serve, spoon yogurt on plate and top with fritters. Garnish with sprinkle of sugar and cinnamon and an additional drizzle of honey.

*Available at most specialty and Middle Eastern markets.
**Available at Cohoctah's Honey Works, see sources, page 248.

LEMON RASPBERRY BREAD PUDDING

SERVES 6 – 8

1 large loaf challah, sliced into 1-inch slices
12 eggs
1½ cups sugar
3 cups heavy whipping cream
3 cups half and half
2¾ teaspoons vanilla
½ teaspoon kosher salt

Lemon Curd (see page 169)
Raspberry and Red Currant Jam (see page 206)
⅓ cup sugar, additional for finishing bread pudding

Additional Lemon Curd
Good quality vanilla ice cream

1 Preheat oven to 350°F.

2 Butter large casserole dish (3½ quart Le Creuset casserole is ideal – or 4 x 10 x 12 inch baking dish)

3 Place bread slices on sheet trays and dry out in oven for about 10 minutes, turning halfway through and being careful not to toast.

4 Beat eggs and sugar together until very well mixed. Add cream, half and half, vanilla, and kosher salt – beat well.

5 Butter pan. Break slices of challah in half and lay out in bottom of pan, forming 1st layer. Break small pieces to fill in cracks if needed. Add 1 cup Lemon Curd in dollops over bread. Spoon 6 to 8 dollops of Raspberry Jam over Lemon Curd.

6 Place a second layer of bread slices over Lemon Curd and Raspberry Jam. Fill in spaces. Dollop 1 cup Lemon Curd over top of bread. Pour egg and cream mixture in each pan to the top of the pan. Let the puddings sit at room temperature for 1 hour.

7 Add more custard to pudding if necessary – bread should be soaked all the way through. Sprinkle with ⅓ cup additional sugar and bake until just set – about 1–1½ hours.

POTS-DE-CRÈME

SERVES 6

This recipe specifies exactly which chocolate we use at the restaurant, but feel free to use your favorite high-quality chocolate.

6 ounces Callebaut semi-sweet chocolate
4 ounces Cuizel 72% dark chocolate
2 ounces El Ray 41% milk chocolate
1¾ cups half and half
6 tablespoons sugar
1 tablespoon instant espresso (we use
   Medaglia d'oro brand)*

Pinch of kosher salt
7 egg yolks
1 teaspoon vanilla

Brown Sugar Cream (see page 161)

1 Chop chocolate.

2 Bring half and half and sugar to just below a simmer in a medium, heavy bottomed saucepan. Add chocolate, whisking until smooth.

3 Add espresso and kosher salt.

4 Whisk yolks just to combine being careful not to over-mix.

5 Ladle chocolate mix into yolks, beating on low – just to incorporate and being careful not to over-mix.

6 Stir in vanilla.

7 Pour through strainer into pitcher, and divide equally into 6 cups.

8 Chill until set, about 4 hours.

9 Garnish with a dollop of Brown Sugar Cream and an additional cupful of Brown Sugar Cream on the side so you can alternate bites.

Available at gourmet grocers.

SUGARED MINT LEAVES

SERVES 12

We always serve these mint leaves to conclude the meal – they are our version of an "after dinner mint" and are very refreshing and rejuvenating after a long hard night of eating.

12 large, hardy mint leaves (As big and in as
      pristine condition as possible.)
1 egg white, whisked just to mix and loosen slightly
¾ cup sugar

1   Prepare small sheet tray lined with parchment paper.

2   Pour sugar onto plate.

3   Place egg white in small mixing bowl or cup and whisk together lightly, just to incorporate.

4   Using a pastry brush, brush mint leaves, one at a time, with egg white coating both sides lightly but evenly.

5   Set mint leaf, one at a time, onto plate with sugar – lift sugar and pour over mint leaf – turn and repeat so mint leaf is thoroughly coated. Place leaves onto prepared sheet tray as you finish – as you lift allow excess sugar to fall off back onto plate.

6   Let mint leaves dry, uncovered, in cool dry place for a minimum of 2 hours.

BRUNCH

FELINO AND EGGS

1 cup or 8 ounces Felino sausage or other delicious cured or smoked sausage, sliced into a long, thin bias
10 large eggs
¼ cup heavy whipping cream
Small splash of cold water
½ teaspoon kosher salt
Freshly ground black pepper

Light olive oil
1½ cups Basil Walnut Pesto (see page 231)
½ baguette, sliced on the bias

Pear Mostarda* (optional, but delicious)

1 In a large mixing bowl combine eggs, heavy cream, a splash cold water, kosher salt and freshly ground black pepper and whisk just to combine.

2 In 1 large or 2 medium non-stick pans heat olive oil/butter over medium-high heat – add sliced felino and sauté briefly – about 45 seconds.

3 Add egg mixture to pan and using rubber spatula gently pull eggs towards center of pan. As they set – reduce heat to medium-low and continue using rubber spatula to pull eggs to center, only as needed.

4 When eggs are just set but still soft, fold in Basil Walnut Pesto gently, adjust seasonings and remove from heat.

5 Serve with warm sliced baguette spread with Pear Mostarda Jam if possible.

Available at Morgan & York's, see sources, page 248.

CHALLAH FRENCH TOAST
WITH SUMMER BERRIES

SERVES 6 – 8

We make this French toast throughout the year finished with whatever fruit is in peak season – it is delicious with sautéed apples, pears and sun dried cherries in the autumn or with fresh peaches and blueberries in the summer – but with ripe summer berries is one of the simplest and best ways to enjoy it.

1 large or 2 medium loaves challah, one day old and cut into 1½-inch thick slices
12 eggs
1 quart heavy cream
¼ cup vanilla
4 tablespoons cinnamon
¾ cup confectioner's sugar

12 slices thick cut bacon (we use Ohio Bacon)*
Vermont maple syrup
salted butter
Light cooking oil
2½ cups summer berries – raspberries, blackberries, blueberries, strawberries

1 Preheat oven to 375°F.

2 Combine eggs, cream, vanilla and then gradually add cinnamon and confectioner's sugar, whisking to combine.

3 Lay bacon out on a sheet tray and cook until just done, about 15 minutes.

4 Pour French toast custard into a deep rectangular pan and soak challah for about 10 minutes per side, until just fully saturated with custard. This step is important so you don't just end up with hot bread instead of the custardy-bread, pudding-like texture French toast is supposed to be.

5 In a large sauté pan over medium-high heat, begin to fry challah in batches in about ½-inch deep oil and butter (about 2 parts oil to one part butter). After a few minutes, when bread is beginning to get crisp and golden, lower the heat to medium-low and continue to cook the first side until deep golden brown and cooked about halfway through – about 6–8 minutes.

6 Flip bread and repeat this process for the other side, beginning with medium-high heat and then lowering to medium-low. You will have to play a little with the heat and pull pan off heat as needed. When finished, the French toast should be a deep golden brown and piping hot throughout.

7 To serve, dress with maple syrup, confectioner's sugar, summer berries and accompany with thick cut bacon.

Available at Sparrow Meats, see sources, page 248.

CHALLAH FRENCH TOAST WITH SUMMER BERRIES

BBQ BEEF SANDWICH ON PUFF PASTRY WITH SPICY COLESLAW AND A FRIED EGG

SERVES 6, WITH LEFTOVERS

½ beef brisket with fat cap,
   about 3½–4 pounds
Kosher salt
Freshly ground black pepper
BBQ Rub (see page 228)
Extra virgin olive oil
BBQ Sauce, one batch (see page 223)

6 large eggs
4 puff pastries (see page 213) or prepared puff
   pastry, or 2 baguettes, sliced into 3 sections
   and split open lengthwise
Spicy Coleslaw (see page 133)

1   Season beef with kosher salt and freshly ground black pepper, and slather with BBQ Rub, coating all sides generously.

2   Cover with film wrap, pressing wrap so it hugs the brisket. Place in non-reactive stainless steel pan and refrigerate for a minimum of 8 hours and up to overnight.

3   Preheat oven to 250°F or heat charcoal grill to medium-low heat.

4   Unwrap brisket and remove excess rub. Season generously with kosher salt and freshly ground black pepper. Sear brisket in olive oil on stove top in heavy duty roasting pan until exterior is caramelized and deep golden brown.

5   Warm BBQ Sauce in separate non-reactive saucepan. Pour into roasting pan, stirring up flavorful bits stuck to bottom of pan. Sauce should come about ⅔ up sides of brisket with top just peeking out (should have some sauce remaining for final preparation).

6   Cover tightly with lid or film wrap and aluminum foil and braise for 4–5 hours or until beef is so tender that it falls apart when checked. Remove from oven and break into chunks.

7   Fry eggs sunnyside up and set aside.

8   To assemble sandwiches, heap BBQ beef onto puff pastries or baguette and top with additional BBQ Sauce, Spicy Coleslaw and finally a fried egg.

SERGIO'S CHICKEN SANDWICH

SERVES 4

While many people who have worked in the restaurant have contributed ideas, concepts or developed recipes for this book, this is the only item actually named after the person who created it. This sandwich is such an integral part of what we actually eat in this restaurant day to day that it seemed it had to be in the restaurant cookbook. Sergio was the first person I hired at the restaurant and has made this sandwich religiously for all of us since the day it opened. It may be the best sandwich you will ever eat – make sure to include as many cilantro stems as possible in your sandwich for the authentic experience.

1 Thai BBQ Chicken (recipe follows)
2 medium, just ripe avocados
2 small or 1 large bunch cilantro leaves and stems
2 small or 1 large ripe Roma tomatoes
⅓ cup (about 15–20 slices) pickled jalapeños

½ cup Sweet Chili Mayonnaise (see page 228)
1 baguette, cut into 4 sections and split open
   lengthwise
Kosher salt

1 Remove roasted chicken from the bone and tear into pieces.

2 To assemble sandwiches spread Sweet Chili Mayonnaise on both sides of interior of bread and layer sliced pickled jalapeños.

3 Fill in the following order with – chicken, cilantro leaves and stems, sliced tomato, avocado and then light sprinkling of kosher salt over avocado.

4 To serve, place other half of baguette on top and press gently to close – cut in half on bias to serve.

THAI BBQ CHICKEN

One 3½ pound chicken
1 quart Thai BBQ Marinade (see page 227)
Kosher salt
Freshly ground black pepper

1 Marinate chicken in 2 cups marinade for 24–36 hours.

2 Place remaining 2 cups marinade in non-reactive, stainless steel saucepan and reduce over low heat until thickened.

3 Remove chicken from marinade and season generously with kosher salt and freshly ground black pepper.

4 Brush generously with reduced sauce and roast until just cooked through – internal temperature should rise above 150°F.

I think we are very lucky to be located in Ann Arbor. Without being on a coast or in a major metropolitan area, Ann Arbor is an unusually rich resource of people growing and producing great food. Just in the restaurant's own historic neighborhood of Kerrytown we are lucky to have TR Durham of Durham's Tracklements whose smoked salmon was named best in the nation by the *New York Times*, Zingerman's Deli, Monahan's Seafood Market, Sparrow Meats and a vibrant farmer's market – several of which have received widespread acclaim as national food treasures. To me, Kerrytown is the kind of special culinary neighborhood you would be excited to find anywhere around the world and I am proud to be a part of the individual character and values that I think Kerrytown represents.

Just a little further out, but still locally, we have John Roos' Roos Roast, Zana Zangana's ZZ's Produce Market, Matt Morgan and Tommy York's Morgan and York, The Croissant Shop where Kurt Boyd hand-makes his unbelievably good puff pastry – and still just a little further, Avalon bakery in Detroit where they bake our delicious, organic bread daily. At the restaurant, we make almost everything from scratch. The items we do not make are those unique ones, we have found, made by people dedicated to creating a limited selection and supply, and which we could not possibly do as well.

Sometimes I wonder what we would do if we didn't have all of these resources – if we couldn't just run across the street to Zingerman's if a customer was interested in some delicious (obscure) ingredient – or call Mike Monahan at home at 9 at night to get permission to get a special fish from his market for a customer. On our part, we are willing to put in the effort, but we are very lucky to be able to have access to these special resources. One of our favorite things is to find these special people who are true artisans in what they do and have the opportunity to get to know them. We are particularly grateful for the support of one person in particular, TR Durham, our neighbor and great friend, who provides us throughout the year with the most incredible hand-cured and smoked fish and meats you will ever taste.

If slow food starts at home then we are very lucky to have this as our home base.

SOFT SCRAMBLED EGGS WITH WASHINGTON STATE TRUFFLES

We were lucky to have a chef friend of ours drop off some black truffles one evening – he stayed for dinner and this is what we made for him to say thank you. It works well as an appetizer as well as a brunch dish.

10 eggs
¼ cup heavy whipping cream
Small splash cold water
Kosher salt
Freshly ground black pepper
Light olive oil

2 small black truffles sliced or shaved paper thin
½ cup Basil Walnut Pesto (see page 231)
2 cups Wild Mushroom Cream (see page 218)
Reggiano Tuile (see page 66)

1 In a large mixing bowl combine eggs, cream, splash of water, kosher salt, freshly ground black pepper and whisk just to combine.

2 Heat in large non-stick pan. Pour in egg mixture and using rubber spatula, gently pull eggs to center as they cook.

3 When eggs are just set but still soft, gently fold in shaved truffles.

4 Spoon warmed Wild Mushroom Cream onto each plate and then place egg and truffle mixture overlapping sauce.

5 Accompany with warm sliced baguettes and a dollop of Basil Walnut Pesto and Reggiano Tuille

SUMMER VEGETABLE SCRAMBLE

SERVES 4

10 large eggs
¼ cup cream
Splash of water
Light cooking oil, for frying
Kosher salt
Freshly ground black pepper
Clarified butter or equal parts butter and light
   cooking oil, as needed
¼ cup red onions, julienned
¼ cup red, yellow or orange peppers, julienned
¼ cup broccoli florets and stalks, cut on the bias,
   blanched in advance for about 2 minutes in
   boiling salted water, shocked in an ice bath
   and strained and dried well

½ cup Fricassee of Wild Mushroom (see page 136)
   (optional)
½ cup smoked mozzarella
½ cup Gouda
½ cup cheddar
½ cup Gruyere
1 Roma tomato, medium dice
1 cup baby spinach

Cilantro Lime Salsa (see page 222)
1 baguette, sliced on the bias

1   In a large mixing bowl combine eggs, cream, splash of water, kosher salt and freshly ground black pepper and whisk just to combine.

2   Heat oil and butter in non-stick pan over medium heat.

3   Add red onion and bell peppers and sauté for a couple of minutes.

4   Add broccoli and Wild Mushroom Fricassee and sauté for about a minute.

5   Add egg mixture to pan and gently fold together eggs and other ingredients.

6   When eggs are just set add cheeses and fold gently into eggs.

7   Fold in tomatoes and spinach, adjust seasonings to taste and remove from heat.

8   Serve with Cilantro Lime Salsa and sliced baguette.

BLUEBERRY PANCAKES

1–1½ cups whole milk
4 tablespoons salted butter, melted
2 large eggs
2 cups all-purpose flour
1 tablespoon plus 1 teaspoon baking powder
¼ cup sugar

1 teaspoon kosher salt
1 cup blueberries
Clarified butter or equal parts butter and light
   cooking oil, as needed
Vermont maple syrup

1 Combine dry ingredients in a large mixing bowl.

2 In separate bowl whisk together milk, melted butter and eggs.

3 Add dry ingredients to wet ingredients and stir together just to combine – being careful not to over-mix – it is okay if some clumps remain in batter.

4 Drop spoonfuls of batter into hot pan with equal parts butter and oil – lightly sprinkle with blueberries and then flip when pancake begins to set and small bubbles are visible on surface. Cook other side until golden and remove to warm platter or sheet tray in a warm place.

5 Eat as soon as humanly possible accompanied with Vermont maple syrup.

CHICKEN SALAD WITH FRUIT AND NUTS

SERVES 6

2 pounds boneless, skinless chicken breast, grilled and seasoned with kosher salt and freshly ground black pepper, cut into medium dice
½ bunch grapes, rinsed and halved lengthwise
2 small stalks celery, fine dice
½ large red onion, fine dice (or 2 small)
1 tablespoone plus 1 teaspoon fresh thyme
1 Granny Smith apple, peeled and small dice
¾–1 cup mayonnaise
½ cup Crème Fraîche (see page 231)

Kosher salt
Freshly ground black pepper to taste
½ cup sliced, blanched almonds, crushed lightly
½ cup walnuts, crushed lightly

Mixed greens
Extra Virgin Olive oil
Sherry vinegar
Baguette, sliced

1 Combine chicken through nuts and adjust seasonings generously to taste.

2 Sprinkle greens with olive oil and vinegar and serve chicken salad alongside greens with sliced baguette.

PAN FRIED TROUT

SERVES 4

4 Ruby trout fillets
Chili Mélange (see page 242)
Chili Mélange Seasoned Flour (see page 244)
Kosher salt
Freshly ground black pepper
Light olive oil
3 cups Tomato Cream (see page 223), warmed
4 slices good grainy, nutty wheat bread

4 large eggs
2 tablespoons freshly chopped herbs, such as flat
   leaf parsley, chives, chervil, basil, thyme – avoiding
   cilantro and rosemary as they may overpower the
   flavor of the other herbs

1 Preheat oven to 400°F.

2 Prepare fish by seasoning generously in the following
   order with kosher salt, freshly ground black pepper
   and Chili Mélange. Dredge in Seasoned Flour and
   shake to remove excess.

3 Heat oil in oven-proof non-stick pan over medium
   high heat.

4 Place fish, presentation side down, in hot pan – sear
   until crisp and golden, turn over, and place in oven
   until fish is just cooked – about 5 minutes.

5 While fish is cooking, toast bread and fry eggs
   sunny side up.

6 To serve, make pool of Tomato Cream and using
   flexible spatula gently place trout over Tomato
   Cream. Top with sunny side up eggs and accompany
   with toasted wheat bread tucking under fish –
   season with kosher salt and freshly ground black
   pepper and chopped fresh herbs.

PAN FRIED TROUT

CUBAN REUBEN

SERVES 4

This sandwich can be made on a sandwich press or panini maker if you have one. Otherwise, a griddle or pan will work fine. According to family stories, I am distantly and vaguely related to the creator of the original Reuben sandwich.

8 challah slices about ¾ inch thick
3 tablespoons salted butter at room temperature
1 cup Sweet Chili Mayonnaise (see page 228)
½ cup cornichons, sliced lengthwise
8 thick cut bacon slices, cooked
  (we use Ohio Bacon)*
½ Marinated Roast Pork Loin or pork tenderloin, sliced thin (recipe follows)

8 ounces Tasso ham, sliced thin
3 ounces Gruyere, sliced
4 eggs

Spicy Roasted Sweet Potatoes (see page 154)

1 Rub 1 side of each challah lightly with butter.

2 Place on grill and slather each piece of bread with Sweet Chili Mayonnaise and then layer in the following order – cornichons, bacon, pork loin, Tasso ham, Gruyere – close sandwich and press top with weight.

3 Meanwhile, cook eggs sunny side up.

4 When bread is deep golden open sandwich just to slide in sunny side up eggs, then reseal.

5 Cut in half and serve with Spicy Roasted Sweet Potatoes and extra Sweet Chili Mayonnaise.

Available at Sparrow Meat, see sources, page 248.

MARINATED ROAST PORK LOIN

1 pound piece of pork loin or pork tenderloin
½ recipe Sweet Chile Marinade (see page 227)
Kosher salt
Freshly ground black pepper
Light cooking oil

1 Marinate pork overnight, tossing well to distribute marinade evenly.

2 Remove from marinade wiping away excess marinade and season generously with kosher salt and freshly ground black pepper.

3 Preheat oven to 400°F.

4 Sear on the stove top in a heavy duty roasting pan over medium-high heat with a little oil just to brown and then transfer to oven to roast until internal temperature reaches 150°F – about 25–30 minutes. Remove from oven and let rest loosely tented in foil for about 15 minutes before slicing.

LAMB FAJITAS

SERVES 4

1½ pounds sirloin of lamb, cut into large cubes
   (about 6 cubes per 8 ounce sirloin)*
Fajita Spice (see page 242)
Kosher salt
Freshly ground black pepper
Extra virgin olive oil
4 large eggs

2 cups Cilantro Lime Salsa (see page 222)
2 cups Slow Cooked Black Beans (see page 145)
1 cup Crème Fraîche (see page 231)
Good quality flour or corn tortillas

1 Season lamb generously with kosher salt and freshly ground black pepper and then rub generously with Fajita Spice rolling meat to coat evenly.

2 Heat extra virgin olive oil in pan over medium-high heat and sear cubed lamb medium rare – about 4 minutes. (While most people do not recommend cooking in extra virgin olive oil, I find that with searing quick-cooking ingredients like this lamb, while you may lose some of the nuance of the oil, it really helps develop beautiful color, texture and richness.)

3 Meanwhile, place tortillas in oven, to warm and fry eggs sunny side up.

4 Serve lamb accompanied with warm Slow Cooked Black Beans, Cilantro Lime Salsa, Crème Fraîche and warm tortillas and fried eggs.

Available through D'artagnan, see sources, page 248.

PICADILLO SANDWICH

SERVES 4

3 cups onions, diced
2 tablespoons garlic, minced
3 tablespoons light olive oil
¾ cups green pepper, small dice
¾ cups red pepper, small dice
2 teaspoons jalapeño, minced
1 teaspoon ground cumin
2 teaspoons oregano
¼ teaspoon plus pinch all spice
¼ teaspoon plus pinch cayenne
1 tablespoon kosher salt
½ teaspoon plus ¼ teaspoon freshly ground black pepper
1 pound ground beef
1 cup Roma tomatoes
½ cup golden raisins
1 teaspoon capers, rough chop

½ cup Spanish olives, rough chop
¼ cup sherry
2½ tablespoons sriracha (we use Shark brand) – or to taste*
1 tablespoon pickled jalapeños, minced
1 teaspoon Worcestershire sauce
1 heaping tablespoon or more to taste brown sugar
½ cup cilantro
½ cup parsley
1 baguette, cut into 4 sections and split lengthwise
4 eggs
Light olive oil, for frying

Carrot Lime Purée (see page 226)
Crème Fraîche (see page 231)
1 avocado, sliced

1 Sauté onions and garlic in olive oil in large sauté pan.

2 Add green and red bell peppers, jalapeño and spices.

3 Add ground beef, brown and strain off excess grease – drain quickly.

4 Add tomatoes, olives, sherry, raisins and capers. Continue cooking for about 5 minutes stirring occasionally. Add sriracha and pickled jalapenos and Worcestershire.

6 Adjust seasonings generously to taste. Turn off heat but keep warm on stovetop.

7 Fry eggs sunnyside up and set aside in warm place.

8 To assemble sandwiches heap picadillo onto baguette and top with fried egg, Carrot Lime Salsa and Crème Fraîche and accompany with sliced avocado.

Available at most Asian markets.

SOUTHWEST TURKEY BURGER

SERVES 4

3 eggs
1 tablespoon extra hot sauce (we use
 Melinda's brand)
¼ cup A-1 sauce
2–3 tablespoons Chili Mélange (see page 242)
1 tablespoons kosher salt
½ teaspoon freshly ground black pepper
2½ pounds fresh ground turkey
1–2 cups fresh bread crumbs or
 soft bread – crumbled

Kosher Salt, additional for seasoning
Freshly ground black pepper, additional
 for seasoning
4 brioche rolls or good quality buns
¾ pound Muenster cheese, cut into thick slices
Light cooking oil, for frying

Cilantro Lime Salsa (see page 222)

1 Combine eggs and seasonings in a large mixing
 bowl until well mixed.

2 Add ground turkey and breadcrumbs to egg
 mixture gently by hand until just combined – being
 careful not to over-mix or meat will bind up and
 become tight.

3 Divide turkey mixture into 4 parts and form very
 gently into patties. Season patties lightly with
 kosher salt and freshly ground black pepper.

4 Cook patties in large, oven-proof sauté pan with oil,
 over medium heat until just cooked through – about
 4 to 5 minutes on each side.

5 Layer Muenster cheese over burger and transfer to
 oven for a few minutes until melted.

6 Serve open faced, on warm brioche or bun and top
 with Cilantro Lime Salsa.

BREAD AND JAM

My mom makes all our jam for us at the restaurant. When the restaurant opened she wanted to find a way to have an ongoing involvement in the restaurant – She is an amazing cook, but my parents live over an hour away so she decided she would learn how to make jam and keep us stocked throughout the year. Now, she has gone crazy with it and makes some of the best jam you will ever eat – we put it in our martinis (Jamtinis), desserts (Polenta Biscuits with homemade jam and Cashel blue cheese) and anything else we can think of. There is no better feeling than to walk into the kitchen at the restaurant and see my mom, talking and laughing with everyone in the kitchen, stirring a big pot of jam with a wooden spoon. She wrote this chapter on Jam to share what she has learned about her new-found passion.

MAKING JAM

Making jam at home can be a challenging experience. Even when the fruit you select looks perfect, it can vary in taste, ripeness and texture – all aspects that will affect the finished product. This caution is not intended to deter you from making jam. Instead, it alerts you to persist with an awareness that you may need to alter the measurements, or vary the ingredients, in order to bring out the best qualities of the fruit that you are working with.

At eve, we have tried to select fruits and berries as they come into their special seasonal ripeness and we often buy them at a local farm stand, or farmers' market where we are familiar with the quality of the produce. We have also purchased fine produce at supermarkets, as long as we selected it carefully. Ideally, we use only fruit, sugar, lemon juice, and possibly a liqueur or condiment that enhances the flavor of a particular jam. Different species of fruit are characterized by different amounts of "pectin,"

a natural substance in fruit that, in combination with the lemon juice and sugar in the recipe, causes the jam to "jell." At the restaurant, we have occasionally used commercially prepared liquid lemon pectin when we were using fruits that were naturally low in pectin, or when jams just did not jell on their own. For those who enjoy the mystery of making jam, it is also possible to prepare home-made pectin-rich "juices" from fruits such as currants, lemons, or crab apples that can be frozen and later added to fruits or berries that have little pectin of their own.

The eight recipes that are included here have produced delicious jams that allow us to serve our own preserves throughout the year in the restaurant. We begin with a number of general guidelines that should make it easier to make good jam and to "repair" jam whose texture is not to your liking. We also review the precautions that should be taken in storing your jam.

1 Examine the fruit to be sure that it is of excellent quality and take care to cut away and discard any part of the fruit that is damaged, overripe, or spoiled.

2 Use only non-reactive utensils for preparing and cooking the jam. Ideally, some combination of stainless steel, glass, wood and/or plastic will prevent discoloration of the fruit.

3 Two methods are available for deciding when the jam has set sufficiently. When you think the jam is ready, remove the pan from the heat and test the temperature with a candy thermometer. A reading of 220°F generally indicates that the mixture is thick enough to jell. Alternatively, spoon a bit of jam on a small plate or saucer and refrigerate for about 2 minutes to chill. The jam has set if it puckers or wrinkles on the surface when you push against it with your fingertip or a spoon. In our jam, we aim to achieve a "soft set" that is neither too liquid, nor too firm. From this perspective, it is just as important to try to avoid overcooking, as to avoid an overly liquid final product.

4 Skim and discard any foam from the jam that accumulates throughout the cooking process, and again when you remove it from the heat after it has set.

5 When the jam is finished, leave it in the pot away from the heat for at least 10 minutes, stirring occasionally to distribute the fruit in the liquid before ladling it into jars. This will help to ensure that the fruit is evenly distributed in the liquid and does not float to the top of the jar.

6 Occasionally, jam does not attain the consistency that you are aiming for on the first try. If it is too thick, you might add enough boiling water to make a somewhat looser spread and then cook it down a bit until if reaches the desired consistency – checking the texture with the thermometer or the cool plate test.

7 If the jam is too thin, one remedy to try is to reprocess it with a small amount of water and sugar and then, after returning the mixture to a boil, to add a tablespoon of liquid lemon pectin per cup of jam and boil rapidly for 1 minute, until it thickens. If this method fails, it is always possible to spoon the thin jam on your bread or biscuit, or use it as a delicious sauce for ice cream, French toast, etc.

Small amounts of jam can be stored in sterilized or very well washed jars in the refrigerator. If you have prepared a larger quantity of jam and plan to store it at room temperature yourself, or are giving it to someone as a gift, you may want to process the jam in a boiling water canner, which will sterilize the jam and preserve its quality for about a year.

The "canning" process involves carefully washing and/or sterilizing the appropriate number of canning jars and covers and having them heated and ready at the same time that you have completed making the jam. The hot jam is ladled into the jars through

a funnel and filled to within ⅛ of an inch of the top of the jar, after which the rim is wiped down with a clean cloth that has been moistened with boiling water. The jars are covered and loosely closed, and then lifted carefully onto a rack in a large canning pot that has been partially filled with boiling water. Additional water is added to cover the jars, which are then processed in boiling water in the covered pan.

The specific time needed to accomplish the processing depends on the size of the jar and the particular type of jam that you are making, but it is typically under 20 minutes. The jars are then removed from the canner and left to cool for 24 hours, after which the special covers are checked to be sure that the process has produced an airtight seal, which protects the purity of the jam. Always remember to label and date each jar of jam at this point so that you can use it in a timely way. Any jars that did not achieve an airtight seal should be processed again, or stored in a refrigerator.

Detailed instructions and explanations of the canning process are presented in most books that deal specifically with making jam and preserving foods. *The Ball Blue Book Guide to Home Canning, Freezing and Dehydration* (2001) is an easily accessed illustrated text that covers the canning process and provides specific instructions on the length of time advised for varied types of jam. It should be consulted for information about the precautions that are advised to insure food safety. At the restaurant, we keep only

a small amount of freshly made jam in the refrigerator and process the remainder in a hot water bath to store for use throughout the year.

The jam recipes we have included are ones that we most enjoy making and serving at eve. They provide a range of experience with a variety of fresh and dried fruits, and should be relatively easy to prepare and enjoy throughout the year. With jam-making, the possibilities are vast. We hope that you enjoy, making, eating, and giving some of these jams.

MAKES ABOUT 4 CUPS, OR 1 QUART OF JAM

1 generous quart Damson plums
¾ cup water
3–4 cups sugar

1   Wash the plums. Cut in half and place the flesh in the jam kettle. Cover the pits with the water and cook in a small pan for about 15 minutes. Strain and add the liquid to the reserved plums, discarding the pits.

2   Measure the fruit mixture that should equal about 4 cups. To each cup of pulp add between ¾ cup to 1 cup of sugar – depending on whether you prefer a more tart or sweeter jam.

3   Place the fruit and sugar mixture in a pan over low heat, stirring carefully with a stainless steel mixing spoon – until the sugar is thoroughly dissolved. Bring to a boil at medium heat and then reduce the heat so that the mixture cooks at a slow simmer.

4   Stir frequently as the liquid evaporates and the mixture thickens – checking to be sure that the sugar does not burn and skimming off any foam that comes to the surface. Within 30–40 minutes the jam should be just about done.

5   Remove the pan from the heat to test with a candy thermometer to see whether the temperature has reached 220°F, or by using the cold plate method discussed previously. Continue cooking and stirring as needed until the jam just reaches the jelling point. Use a stainless steel spoon, to skim off any foam that has accumulated on the top and sides of the pan.

6   Ladle the hot jam into the sterilized jars that you have prepared for this purpose. Process in a boiling water canner for the time appropriate to the type and quantity of jam that you have made, or cool to room temperature and store in the refrigerator. Remember to label and date each jar of jam that you make.

For best results, use locally grown strawberries at the peak of their season. Strawberries, and other fruits and berries that are available out of season, may have been developed to resist spoilage and for easy transport, but be less tender and juicy than seasonal local fruits and therefore less suited to making tasty jam.

2 quarts of fresh strawberries (about 2 pounds)
6 cups sugar
3 tablespoon freshly squeezed lemon juice

2 teaspoons cardamon pods, optional, wrapped and tied in cheesecloth

1   Wash, drain, and hull the strawberries. Discard any that are overripe and add more good quality berries to top off the quart measure.

2   Carefully layer the strawberries in a non-reactive bowl or kettle, alternating a layer of berries with a layer of the sugar. Cover and allow to stand overnight. The berries should have released an ample amount of liquid by the next day.

3   Add 3 tablespoons of lemon juice to the mixture and stir gently. Transfer the contents of the bowl into your jam kettle and bring to a boil over low heat. Add bundle of cardamom seeds if desired and simmer for about 10 minutes, stirring occasionally, until the mixture is quite clear.

4   Transfer the mixture to the bowl, cover, and allow to stand for another 24 hours. Again, return to the pan and cook over medium heat for about 20 minutes, stirring and skimming occasionally.

5   When the liquid appears to have thickened, remove the pan from the heat. Remove the pan from the burner and, using a stainless steel spoon, gently skim any foam that has accumulated on the top and sides of the pan.

6   Allow the mixture to cool somewhat, stirring occasionally so that the preserved berries are distributed throughout the surrounding syrup.

7   Ladle the jam into sterilized jars that you have prepared for this purpose. Process in a boiling water canner for the time appropriate for the type and quantity of jam that you have prepared, or cool to room temperature and store in the refrigerator. Remember to label and date each jar of jam that you make.

FRESH APRICOT JAM

After making this jam, we have sometimes found small fibers from the skin or flesh in on finished product. Feel free to strain the jam through a non-reactive strainer as needed. It will still taste delicious.

3½ pounds apricots
1½ cups water

2 tablespoons freshly squeezed lemon juice
6 cups sugar

1   Wash the apricots and cut them in half. Discard the pits but do not peel the fruit. Place the apricots, water and lemon juice in your jam kettle and bring to a boil. Simmer for about 30 minutes, stirring occasionally. The fruit should be tender and the liquid reduced by about a third.

2   Add the sugar – stirring well to incorporate it thoroughly into the fruit mixture. Bring to a boil over medium heat and then boil rapidly for about 15 minutes. Stir occasionally being careful to prevent the jam at the bottom of the pan from burning.

3   Reduce to a gentle simmer and continue cooking and stirring as needed just until the jam reaches the jelling point. Remove the pan from the burner and, using a stainless steel spoon, gently skim any foam that has accumulated on the top and sides of the pan. Test the mixture with a candy thermometer to see whether the temperature has reached 220°F on a candy thermometer, or by using the cold plate method discussed previously. Repeat the process of skimming and testing just until the desired consistency has been reached – about 30 minutes.

4   Ladle the jam into the warm sterilized jars that you have prepared beforehand for this purpose. Process in a boiling water canner for the time appropriate for the type and quantity of jam that you have prepared, or cool to room temperature and store in the refrigerator. Remember to label and date each jar of jam that you make.

BLUEBERRY AMARETTO JAM

MAKES ABOUT 1 QUART OF JAM

4 cups fresh blueberries
4 cups sugar
3 tablespoons freshly squeezed lemon juice

About 3 tablespoons of Amaretto liqueur,
   or to taste.

1 Wash and then drain the blueberries. Place berries, sugar, and lemon juice in a large non-reactive bowl. Stir gently to combine, using a non-reactive spoon, and allow to stand for 2–3 hours – stirring occasionally to incorporate contents of the bowl.

2 Transfer the ingredients to your jam kettle and bring to a boil, stirring gently. Allow the mixture to boil for about 15 minutes, stirring occasionally to prevent the bottom from burning.

3 As the jam thickens, remove the pan from the heat periodically and test with a candy thermometer to see whether the temperature has reached 220°F, or by using the cold plate method discussed previously. Continue cooking, until the jam has set to a soft jell.

4 When the jam is done use a stainless steel spoon and gently skim any remaining foam that has accumulated on the surface. Stir in 2½ tablespoons of Amaretto liqueur and cook the jam for another minute. Ladle the jam into the warm sterilized jars that you have prepared beforehand for this purpose. Process in a boiling water canner for the time appropriate for the type and quantity of jam that you have prepared, or cool to room temperature and store in the refrigerator. Remember to label and date each jar of jam that you make.

RASPBERRY AND RED CURRANT JAM

MAKES ABOUT 1 QUART OF JAM

If you have a source of red currants, ideally from an organic producer, you can prepare red currant juice ahead of time and freeze it for use throughout the year. Currant juice that is prepared commercially does not provide the pectin that is useful in promoting jelling of fruits such as raspberries and tart cherries.

3 cups red raspberries
½ cup water
1½ cups Red Currant Juice (recipe follows)
About 3 cups sugar
1 tablespoon freshly squeezed lemon juice

1   Bring the raspberries and water to a boil and cook over medium heat for about 10 minutes. Stir occasionally until the fruit is tender.

2   If you wish, strain about half of the raspberries to reduce the amount of seeds in the final product.

3   Place the cooked raspberries, currant juice, sugar, and lemon juice in a non-reactive pot.

4   Bring to a boil and cook for about 20 minutes, or until the mixture begins to thicken. Remove the pan from the heat periodically and test with a candy thermometer to seer whether the temperature has reached 220°F, or by using the cold plate method discussed previously. Continue cooking, until the jam has set to a soft jell.

5   When the jam is done use a stainless steel spoon and gently skim any remaining foam that has accumulated on the surface. Allow the jam to cool in the pan so that the fruit are distributed evenly throughout the mixture and do not float to the top. Ladle the jam into the warm sterilized jars that you have prepared beforehand for this purpose. If you plan to store the jam at room temperature, it should be processed in a boiling-water canner. Alternatively, cool the jars to room temperature and then refrigerate.

RED CURRANT JUICE

1 generous quart of red currants, about 1½ pounds
2½ cups of water

1   Remove the currants from their stems and wash and drain them. If they have been grown organically, you can be more comfortable about leaving some of the stems on the fruit. Place the currants and the water in a non-reactive pan. Bring to a boil stirring and then boil for about 10 minutes – until the mixture is quite juicy.

2   Strain the mixture through a non-reactive fine strainer, which you may line with special culinary cheesecloth. Measure the juice, which should produce just about 2 cups. The juice can be stored in the refrigerator or freezer for use later in the season.

This recipe may benefit from the addition of commercially-prepared lemon pectin.

An orchard in our area grows tart cherries and pits and freezes them in 5 or 10 pound containers without any sugar or other additives. When cherries are out of season, we use these cherries in making this jam, and have found that the commercially produced liquid lemon pectin can be very helpful in promoting jelling since tart cherries are a fruit that has little natural pectin.

3 pounds pitted fresh tart cherries, or frozen
   tart cherries, pitted partially thawed.
About 4½ cups sugar
1¼ cups water

2 tablespoons freshly squeezed lemon juice
1 packet commercially prepared lemon pectin
   extract, if needed

1 Bring cherries, lemon juice, and water to a boil and cook rapidly for about 10 minutes. Add sugar and stir until completely dissolved. Boil, stirring occasionally for about 20–25 minutes, or until the mixture begins to thicken. Skim as necessary.

2 Remove the pan from the heat periodically and test with a candy thermometer to see whether the temperature has reached 220°F, or by using the cold plate method discussed previously. Continue cooking until the jam has set to a soft jell.

3 If the jam does not appear to be jelling, add a packet of liquid lemon pectin, stirring rapidly as you bring the mixture to a boil. Boil rapidly for 1 minute and the mixture should jell.

4 When the jam is done, use a stainless steel spoon and gently skim any remaining foam that has accumulated on the surface. Allow the jam to cool in the pan for at 10 or more minutes so that the cherries are distributed evenly throughout the liquid and do not float to the top.

5 Ladle the jam into the warm sterilized jars that you have prepared beforehand for this purpose. If you plan to store the jam at room temperature, it should be processed in a boiling-water canner. Alternatively, cool the jars to room temperature and then refrigerate. Remember to label and date each jar of jam that you make.

COOKING WITH AN OPEN MIND

Growing up, my mom never followed a recipe, which gave me a model for a certain kind of freedom. She would often start out with a recipe, but would never hesitate to substitute ingredients freely until it ended up with a result that was always delicious, but not often resembling what it was intended to be. She never really brought me into the kitchen to give me formal instruction on how to cook, but being around real food – just spending time in the kitchen – eating family dinner every night – I kind of learned to cook almost through osmosis. My most vivid memories are of smells or images of the food we ate, even the bowl something was served in – even if it was just a bowl of spaghetti and meat sauce – everything always tasted delicious.

For me, there is a foundation of organization that is important to have in place in cooking and the rest should be free-spirited. This includes starting with a clean workspace, gathering your ingredients and equipment together before you begin and following proper technique. If you make the effort to do these things, you actually have a lot more freedom to be spontaneous with your cooking while you are doing it. Using proper technique eliminates a lot of room for error and you can concentrate fully on your ingredients and the flavors and consistency of your food as it develops. There are always little surprises that can come up in cooking, so having the foundation in place, you will have the confidence, time and resilience to work through them as they come up.

Once this organization is in place, you can really be open-minded with your cooking. It is good to follow recipes, but not blindly. Use your senses – if you are really paying attention to the look and feel of the food, you have the best chance of getting the most delicious result. When we make the Cilantro Lime Salsa in late August when tomatoes are at their peak in Michigan it is very different than making the same recipe in March. If you look at the salsa you will notice it is paler and thinner. Without the rich juice of the tomatoes, the spices will become more prominent. In October, you may decide to just cut back on the spices and in December, to use canned or preserved tomatoes – or, probably the best choice, to wait until next summer when tomatoes are at their prime. By really looking at the food, even without tasting it you will develop the ability to see what is going on with whatever you are working on. When I walk through the kitchen at the restaurant, I feel like I am tasting things as I walk by, just by really looking at them as I pass by. If the salsa looks pale, more watery, I know that the tomatoes were not ripe enough or, if the Pots de Crème looks darker, I know that it likely does not have enough cream and will be more dense than it should be.

Especially with tasting, it is important to be open-minded and see where it leads you. Take your time and don't let yourself feel rushed. I am a very decisive person, but when I am tasting I get really into it and the taste lingers in my mind – sometimes it takes an extra few minutes to realize what something really needs.

Often, when one of the cooks asks me what I think a certain dish needs – there is a delayed reaction – the taste lingers – a minute or two later it is still in my mind – and then it comes to me exactly what it needs – salt – thyme – a certain spice. It sounds crazy, and not very efficient, but there are times when we spend 45 minutes seasoning or finishing a single sauce or a soup in the kitchen. But, you know the difference when something is good, but not quite right – then it might even go backwards – but if you remain calm – adjust and tweak it – and all of a sudden it comes around and is absolutely delicious – and that is definitely worth it. In a restaurant you may be making 4 quarts of a sauce and then that extra few moments makes the difference between it being okay, good or great for the next 20 guests.

DRIED APRICOT JAM
WITH CRYSTALLIZED GINGER

MAKES 8 CUPS OF JAM

4 cups dried apricots
9 cups water
7 cups sugar

5 tablespoons freshly squeezed lemon juice
½ cup finely chopped crystallized ginger

1   Cut all of the apricots into quarters. Place half of the apricots in 4½ cups of water and store overnight covered in a non-reactive container. Reserve the remaining apricots.

2   In a large non-reactive pot, combine the apricots that have been soaking in the water, the reserved apricots, an additional 4½ cups water, and the lemon juice. Bring to a boil and simmer for about 40 minutes, until the apricots are quite soft. Stir occasionally with a stainless steel cooking spoon.

3   Add the 7 cups of sugar and stir carefully over low heat – until the sugar is thoroughly dissolved. Bring to a boil at medium heat and continue to boil for 10–12 minutes, stirring occasionally. Skim the surface of the jam to remove any foam or impurities from the jam.

4   Remove the pan from the heat periodically and test with a candy thermometer to see whether the temperature has reached 220°F, or by using the cold plate method discussed previously. Continue cooking until the jam has set to a soft jell.

5   When the jam has reached the desired consistency add the chopped crystallized ginger and stir well to incorporate.

6   Ladle the jam into the warm sterilized jars that you have prepared beforehand for this purpose. If you plan to store the jam at room temperature, it should be processed in a boiling-water canner. Alternatively, cool the jars to room temperature and then refrigerate. Remember to label and date each jar of jam that you make.

DRIED MISSION FIG AND ORANGE SPREAD WITH COGNAC

MAKES ABOUT 1 QUART

1 pound dried mission figs
2 cups boiling water
¾ cup sugar
1 cup freshly squeezed orange juice, including pulp

1 tablespoon grated orange peel
2 tablespoons Cognac, to taste

1 Remove stems from figs with a paring knife. Cut each fig in half and then slice into 6–8 pieces, depending on size of fig.

2 Place prepared figs in a mixing bowl. Cover figs with about 1 cup of boiling water and allow to soak for at least 1 hour, or until soft. Place figs in the jam kettle and bring to a slow simmer for about 15–20 minutes, until figs are tender and water has just about evaporated.

3 Add 12 tablespoons sugar and 1½ cups of orange juice and stir gently. Cook for about 20 minutes until the sugar has dissolved and the orange juice has cooked into the figs. Remove from heat and stir in 1 tablespoon grated orange peel, and 3 tablespoons of cognac, if desired. Return to the stove and simmer for another minute or two.

4 Cool spread to room temperature and then refrigerate. Remember to label and date each jar of jam that you make.

POLENTA BISCUITS

MAKES 6 LARGE BISCUITS

½ cup plus 2 tablespoons finely ground cornmeal*
½ cup plus 2 tablespoons flour
3 tablespoons plus 1 teaspoon sugar
1½ teaspoons baking powder
1 teaspoon salt

1 egg
¾ cup plus 1 tablespoon half and half
⅔ stick salted butter, melted, cooled to room temperature

1 Preheat oven to 350°F.

2 Lightly grease 6 of the 12 cups of a large 1 cup measure muffin tin.

3 Combine dry ingredients in a large bowl and make a well in the center.

4 Combine liquid ingredients in a separate mixing bowl.

5 Pour liquids into well, and stir until barely combined.

6 Spoon batter into muffin tins and bake until just set and golden – about 15 to 20 minutes.

*Available through Zingerman's Deli, see sources, page 248.

This recipe is adapted from Craig Claiborne's Southern Cooking. His New York Times International Cookbook was the first cookbook I owned and fell in love with when I was about 12 years old. He had an awesome knack for collecting authentic and extremely delicious recipes from all over the world and these traditional southern biscuits baked in muffin tins are a great example.

2¼ cups all-purpose flour
½ teaspoon kosher salt, ground finer between finger tips
3 tablespoons plus 1 teaspoon sugar
1½ teaspoons baking powder

1½ sticks salted butter, cut into tablespoons at room temperature
½ cup buttermilk
½ cup heavy whipping cream

1 Preheat oven to 350°F.

2 Lightly grease muffin tins with salted butter.

3 Sift together the flour, kosher salt, sugar and baking powder into a mixing bowl.

4 Use your fingers or a pastry cutter to work the butter into the dry ingredients until it has a sandy texture. Add the cream and buttermilk into well and stir to just blend, being extremely careful not to over-mix or biscuits will become tough.

5 Spoon the mixture into a lightly greased muffin tin pan with 24 indentations. Bake until just set and crusty and golden brown on top – about 30–40 minutes.

PUFF PASTRY

3½ cups unbleached all-purpose flour
1 cup cold water
5 tablespoons unsalted butter, melted

2 teaspoons salt
1½ cups unsalted butter

1 Sift flour onto chilled work surface and make a well in center – add water, melted butter and salt. Mix together with fingertips.

2 Using a pastry scraper, work flour and butter mixture until loose crumbles form – add more water if dough seems dry.

3 Shape dough into a ball. Cut an "x" on top to prevent shrinkage. Wrap in floured parchment and chill for 30 minutes.

4 Remove from refrigerator and on a chilled and lightly floured surface flatten ball and roll out to form a cross, leaving a mound in the center.

5 Place the butter square in the center of the cross. Fold over each section, pulling the dough slightly to completely enclose the butter.

6 Lightly flour the work surface and roll over the top of the dough to seal the edges, then fold the dough into a rectangle.

7 Roll the dough into a 8 x 18 inch rectangle. Fold the bottom third up toward the middle.

8 Bring the top third of the dough over the folded thirds, and brush off any excess flour.

9 The dough should be square, have three layers and the edges should align – now the dough needs turning.

10 Give the square a quarter turn so that the exposed edge is on your right, as if the dough were a book. Gently press the edges to seal.

11 Roll the dough into an 8 x 18 inch rectangle. Fold it again into thirds – seal edges. Chill for 30 minutes. Repeat rolling, folding and turning twice more.

12 To bake, roll dough out to about ¼-inch in thickness. Cut into desired size and prick all over with a fork. Brush tops with egg wash, being careful not to let egg wash come too close to the edges or it will run down and prevent the puffs from rising properly. Bake at 375°F until puffed and golden, about 20–30 minutes.

SAUCES

MANGO CREAM

MAKES ABOUT 2 CUPS

2 cups heavy whipping cream
½ cup whole garlic cloves
2 tablespoons hot mango chutney (we use Pataks brand or we make Exotic Fruit Chutney, page 219, when fruit is in peak season)*
2 tablespoons sweet mango chutney (we use Pataks brand or we make Exotic Fruit Chutney, page 219, when fruit is in peak season)
1 tablespoon sweet chili sauce (we use Mae Ploy brand)**

1 Combine garlic and heavy whipping cream in non-reactive pan and simmer gently for about 20 minutes – cream should be thickened slightly and the garlic should be very soft.

2 Remove from heat – strain – pressing garlic into sieve with the back of a ladle to extract as much flavor as possible (discard remaining garlic).

3 Add remaining ingredients to cream – stirring to combine.

*Available at most Indian markets or gourmet grocers.
**Available at most Asian markets.

MUSTARD CREAM

MAKES ABOUT 1½ CUPS

1 cup Crème Fraîche (see page 231)
2½ tablespoons honeycup mustard
2 tablespoons whole grain mustard
½ teaspoon kosher salt
¼ cup heavy cream

Combine all ingredients.

CURRY CREAM

MAKES ABOUT 1 QUART

- 2 tablespoons salted butter
- 3 tablespoons light olive oil
- 3 cups yellow onion, minced
- 4 tablespoon ginger, minced
- 3 tablespoons garlic, minced
- 2 tablespoons jalapeño, minced, or to taste
- 2 teaspoons hot curry powder*
- 2 teaspoons sweet curry powder*
- 1 teaspoon coriander
- 2 teaspoons turmeric
- Pinch of cayenne
- 1 tablespoon kosher salt or more to taste
- ½ teaspoon freshly ground black pepper, to taste
- 1 quart heavy whipping cream
- 1 teaspoon sriracha or to taste, (we use Shark brand)**
- 2 teaspoons lime juice or to taste
- 1 tablespoon brown sugar or to taste
- Heaping ½ cup Parmigiano Regianno or aged provolone, grated (we use equal parts of each), or more to taste

1. Heat oil and butter in large saucepan and sauté onions, ginger, garlic, and jalapeños for about 3 minutes.

2. Season with spices and salt and pepper.

3. Add cream, simmer to reduce until sauce thickens, but is still silky and coats the back of a spoon – about 30–40 minutes.

4. Remove from heat – add sriracha, lime juice, and brown sugar and cheese.

5. Adjust seasonings generously to taste.

Available through Penzeys, see sources, page 248.
**Available at most Asian markets.*

CÈPE CREAM

MAKES ABOUT 4 QUARTS

- 3 tablespoons fresh shallots, minced
- 3 tablespoons fresh garlic, minced
- 3 pounds cèpes or favorite assortment of wild and cultivated mushrooms
- 1 tablespoon kosher salt
- Freshly ground black pepper
- 1⅓ cups sherry (we use Lustau Amontillado Sherry)
- 6 cups Chicken Essence (see page 68) stock or broth (If using broth, use College Inn brand.)
- 1 quart heavy whipping cream
- 1 quart sour cream
- 2 cups Parmigiano Reggiano or aged provolone, grated, (At the restaurant, we use equal parts of each.)
- 1 cup fresh herbs, chopped such as flat leaf parsley, chives, chervil, basil, thyme avoiding cilantro and rosemary as they may overpower the flavor of the other herbs

Crème Fraîche (see page 231), for garnish

1. Sweat shallots and garlic with some kosher salt over medium-low heat.

2. Add mushrooms and raise heat to medium-high until mushrooms exude liquid. Simmer until liquid is almost completely gone. Season generously with kosher salt and freshly ground black pepper.

3. Deglaze with sherry and cook for a few minutes, or until sherry is incorporated with mushrooms.

4. Add chicken stock and cream and reduce until mixture thickens and coats the back of a spoon – about 20–30 minutes.

5. Temper with sour cream by adding some of the sauce to the sour cream and then adding sour cream back into the sauce.

6. Simmer until slightly thickened.

7. Add cheese and fresh herbs, adjust seasonings and then immediately remove from heat.

8. Garnish with Crème Fraîche.

WILD MUSHROOM CREAM

MAKES ABOUT 2 QUARTS

We make this sauce throughout the year with different mushrooms as they come into their prime season. It is amazing to see how the flavor changes from using chanterelles to cèpes to hedgehogs, etc… It is also absolutely delicious, however, with any combination of mushrooms readily available at the market – shiitakes, portabellas, crimini and button.

1½ tablespoons fresh shallots, minced
1½ tablespoons fresh garlic, minced
Light olive oil
1½ pounds assorted, wild, cultivated mushrooms, sliced or torn into equivalent sized pieces
1–2 teaspoons kosher salt
Freshly ground black pepper
⅔ cup sherry (we use Lustau Amontillado Sherry)
3 cups Chicken Essence (see page 68) stock or broth (If using canned chicken broth, use College Inn brand.)
2 cups heavy whipping cream
2 cups sour cream
1 cup Parmigiano Reggiano or aged provolone, grated, (we use equal parts of each)
¾ cup fresh herbs, chopped, such as flat leaf parsley, chives, chervil, basil, thyme avoiding cilantro and rosemary as they may overpower the flavor of the other herbs

Crème Fraîche (see page 231), for garnish

1   In shallow braising pan or stock pot sweat shallots and garlic with olive oil and a light sprinkling of kosher salt on medium-low heat.

2   Add mushrooms and raise heat to medium-high until mushrooms exude liquid. Simmer until liquid is almost completely gone. Season generously with kosher salt and freshly ground black pepper.

3   Deglaze with sherry and cook for a few minutes, or until sherry is incorporated with mushrooms.

4   Add chicken stock and cream and reduce until mixture thickens and coats the back of a spoon – about 20–30 minutes.

5   Temper with sour cream by adding some of the sauce to the sour cream and then adding sour cream back into the sauce.

6   Simmer until slightly thickened.

7   Add cheese and fresh herbs, adjust seasonings and then immediately remove from heat.

FRESH MINT CHUTNEY

MAKES ABOUT 2 CUPS

1 cup cilantro leaves, packed
1 cup mint, packed
1 cup dried unsweetened coconut
10 garlic cloves
¼ cup plus 2 teaspoons lemon juice
2 tablespoons ginger, minced
2 cups scallions, sliced
1 large jalapeño, seeds removed
1 teaspoon kosher salt

Place all ingredients in food processor and purée.

EXOTIC FRUIT CHUTNEY

We make this dish with all different kinds of fruit throughout the seasons – lychees, rambutan, star fruit – just remember to add the more delicate fruit towards the end.

1 tablespoon light cooking oil
1 ripe golden pineapple, cored and medium dice
½ red bell peppers, fine dice
½ red onion, fine dice
½ jalapeño, seeds removed and minced
3 tablespoons Vermont maple syrup
2 tablespoons dark rum
1 teaspoon sriracha (we use Shark brand)*
⅓ cup rice wine vinegar (we use Marukan unseasoned)
½ cup plus one tablespoon brown sugar
2 tablespoons sweet chili sauce (we use Mae Ploy brand)*
2 mangoes
1¼ cups kumquats, sliced

¼ bunch mint chiffonade, (ribbon cut)
¼ bunch cilantro

1 Quickly sauté pineapple, bell peppers, onions and chilies with light oil in a non-reactive pan.

2 Add remaining ingredients except mangoes, kumquats, and herbs. Simmer until just softened, about 15 minutes. Add mangoes and kumquats, stir to combine, and adjust seasonings.

3 Remove from heat and let cool completely. Add herbs only when chutney has completely cooled.

*Available at most Asian markets.

SMOKEY TOMATO SALSA

5 Roma tomatoes
Extra virgin olive oil
Kosher salt
¼ bunch cilantro, rough chop
¼ teaspoon ground cumin
2 teaspoons fresh garlic, minced
1 chipotle pepper, canned in adobo sauce, or more to taste (we use San Marcos brand)
Kosher salt, to taste
Freshly ground black pepper, to taste

1 Drizzle tomatoes with extra virgin olive oil, sprinkle with kosher salt and grill or roast until soft and blistered in 450°F oven.

2 Place in food processor and purée all ingredients – adjust seasonings generously.

CILANTRO LIME SALSA

MAKES ABOUT 5 CUPS

Because tomatoes vary so much with the season, it is important to look at and taste dishes like this salsa carefully. In the summer, when tomatoes are juicier, of course they will contribute a lot more flavor and depth to the salsa. When they are not in peak season, the spices come through more powerfully, so you may have to cut back slightly on the spices. After a while, you will be able to look at the color and body and determine what it may need, before even tasting it. At the restaurant, we try to stick to highlighting tomatoes, and most ingredients, when they are at their best – but this is one dish that you can make later in the year than most. As the tomatoes macerate in the fresh lime juice, salt and olive oil, they pick up incredible flavor. When finding good tomatoes starts to become a challenge, customers at the restaurant always ask us where we are still finding good ones when they eat this salsa.

8 Roma tomatoes, medium dice
1 bunch scallions, thinly sliced at a bias
½ bunch cilantro leaves, rough chop
1 tablespoon garlic, minced
½ jalapeño peppers, seeds removed and minced
2 teaspoons fresh lime juice
1 teaspoon extra virgin olive oil
1 tablespoon Chili Mélange (see page 242)
2 teaspoons kosher salt

Combine all and adjust seasoning generously.

CHIMICHURRI

MAKES ABOUT 2 CUPS

5 large cloves garlic, smashed
½ teaspoon bay leaves, ground in spice mill or coffee grinder
2 jalapeño peppers, seeds removed and coarse chop
1 teaspoon kosher salt
¼ teaspoon white pepper
1½ cups curly parsley, coarse chop
1½ cups flat leaf parsley, coarse chop
¼ cup fresh oregano, fine chop
¼ cup distilled white vinegar
¼ cup plus 2 tablespoons extra virgin olive oil

1 In a food processor purée garlic, bay leaves, jalapeños and kosher salt and white pepper.

2 Add parsley and oregano, processing to blend well.

3 Gradually add oil in a slow, steady stream while food processor is running to emulsify. Add vinegar, taste and adjust seasonings. Allow sauce to rest for at least 2 hours before using to allow flavors to meld.

BBQ SAUCE

MAKES 4 QUARTS

You can use this barbecue sauce to braise anything from spareribs to beef brisket to pork shoulder – it makes pretty much any slow-cooked barbecue taste delicious.

6 tablespoons vegetable oil
3 large red onions, rough chop
¾ cup fresh garlic, minced
¾ cup plus 2 teaspoons light brown sugar, packed
2 tablespoons smoked paprika
1½ cups cider vinegar
2¼ cups molasses
3 tablespoons Worcestershire sauce
Three 28 ounce cans crushed tomatoes
¾ cup puréed chipotles in adobo, puréed (we use San Marcos brand)
½ cup plus 1 tablespoon mustard
6 bay leaves
¾ extra hot sauce (we use Melinda's brand)
1½ cups Heinz ketchup
2 tablespoons kosher salt
Freshly ground black pepper

1 Sauté onions in oil until soft in large, non-reactive saucepan.

2 Add garlic, stirring to just incorporate.

3 Add sugar, stirring as it begins to caramelize.

4 Stir in paprika and then cider vinegar.

5 Add remaining ingredients and simmer until thickened, about 45 minutes. Adjust seasonings and remove bay leaves before using.

TOMATO CREAM

MAKES ABOUT 6 CUPS

½ cup light olive oil
2 yellow onions
12 garlic cloves, sliced paper thin lengthwise
2½ teaspoons kosher salt
2 teaspoons freshly ground black pepper
¼ cup fresh thyme
1 carrot, finely shredded
⅓ cup sherry (we use Lustau Amontillado Sherry)
Four 28 ounce cans whole tomatoes (we use Dei Fratelli brand)
1 teaspoon crushed red pepper
1½ cups heavy whipping cream
3 tablespoons Fresh Herb Butter (see page 33)
1 cup Parmigiano Reggiano, shredded
1 cup aged provolone, shredded
½ cup mixed chopped fresh herbs such as flat leaf parsley, chives, chervil, basil, thyme avoiding cilantro and rosemary as they may overpower flavor of other herbs

1 Heat olive oil in a large, non-reactive saucepan or stockpot over medium heat. Add onions, garlic, kosher salt and freshly ground black pepper – cook until soft and just golden, stirring frequently.

2 Add thyme and carrots and cook until soft.

3 Deglaze with sherry.

4 Add tomatoes with their juice and crushed red pepper. Bring to a boil – then reduce to a simmer. Simmer gently until slightly thickened.

5 Add heavy cream and continue to simmer until thickened – it should taste very rich and flavorful.

6 Finish by adding Fresh Herb Butter, cheeses and remaining fresh herbs. Adjust seasonings generously to taste.

THE BLUEBERRY TEST

The first day we held interviews for the restaurant was a really beautiful day in late summer. Nichole, our dining room manager, and I went to the farmer's market around the corner and came back with a quart of perfect, plump blueberries. We were eating them when the first person arrived for his interview and so of course, we asked him if he wanted some blueberries. Throughout the day we had to make several trips back to the farmer's market because the blueberries were just so good, we kept going through them – it's hard to stop eating Michigan blueberries in July.

After a long day, we met to review how we felt about all of the people we had interviewed – to analyze their strengths, weaknesses, experience and all of the things you are supposed to look for in a job candidate. We found that we had the same favorite people – all of whom we had felt immediately comfortable with. I had noticed and finally, quietly confessed, that it seemed like all of the people we liked so much were the people who were the most excited about the blueberries. Nichole exclaimed that she had been thinking the exact same thing all day.

I don't know that there is a scientific correlation between the people the most excited about, and most voraciously eating the blueberries and who makes a good job candidate – But, I honestly believe that there is a basic bond and connection between people who are passionate about food – no matter what their background or job experience. Those are the people that turned out to be a natural fit at the restaurant and really lasted. How they felt about food continued on to their passion for life and natural warmth as a person.

CARROT LIME PURÉE

Many cultures and cuisines make a variation of this sauce, but this recipe is adapted from Steve Raichlen's Miami Spice Cookbook. It is extremely flavorful and versatile and seems like it goes with just about anything.

1 green bell pepper, rough chop
1 cup onions, rough chop
¾ cup fresh lime juice
½ cup light olive oil
1 pound carrots, peeled and ½-inch sliced
10–12 cloves garlic
1–2 teaspoons sugar
⅛–¼ cup water
Kosher salt
Freshly ground black pepper

1 Place bell peppers, onions, olive oil and lime juice in food processor.

2 Slowly add olive oil while food processor is running to emulsify.

3 Add carrots, garlic and sugar.

4 Add a small amount of water if necessary to loosen up sauce and season with kosher salt and freshly ground black pepper.

LEMON GRASS MARINADE

MAKES ABOUT 2 CUPS

8 shallots, sliced
8 garlic cloves, sliced
¾ cup lemon grass, minced
¼ cup fish sauce
¼ cup soy sauce (we use Kikkoman brand)
1 teaspoon kosher salt
¼ cup sugar
¼ cup light cooking oil

1 Combine first 2 ingredients in mortar and pestle or food processor and blend to a paste.

2 Transfer to a mixing bowl and add the lemon grass, fish sauce, soy sauce, salt, and sugar – add oil in a slow, steady stream whisking to emulsify.

AROMATIC ASIAN MARINADE

MAKES ABOUT 2 CUPS

½ cup sweet chili sauce (we use Mae Ploy brand)*
½ cup mango chutney (we use Major Grey brand)*
¼ cup soy sauce (we use Kikkoman brand)*
2 tablespoons stone ground whole grain mustard
¼ cup fresh garlic, minced
1½ teaspoons Chili Mélange (see page 242)
1 tablespoon five spice
½ teaspoon freshly ground black pepper
3 tablespoons hoisin sauce (we use Koon Chun brand)*
3 tablespoons Asian BBQ Sauce (we use Koon Chun brand)*
2 teaspoons brown sugar to taste

Combine all ingredients.

Available at most Asian markets.

SWEET CHILI MARINADE

MAKES ABOUT 2½ CUPS

½ cup Chili Oil (see page 236) or ½ cup light olive oil and a pinch of ground habanero chilies
½ cup brown sugar
½ cup hoisin sauce (we use Koon Chun brand)*
8 ounces pineapple juice
1 teaspoon ground cumin
¼ cup cilantro, rough chop

Combine all.

Available at most Asian markets.

THAI BBQ MARINADE

MAKES ABOUT 4 CUPS

¼ cup sesame oil
½ cup Thai sweet chili sauce (we use Mae Ploy brand)*
2 cups sherry (we use Lustau Amontillado Sherry)*
¼ cup soy sauce (we use Kikkoman brand)*
1 heaping cup peanut butter
¼ cup sriracha (we use Shark brand)*
¼ cup fresh ginger, minced
2 tablespoons garlic, minced

Combine all ingredients except sesame oil in non-reactive mixing bowl. Add sesame oil gradually while whisking to incorporate.

Available at most Asian markets.

40 CLOVES OF GARLIC MARINADE

MAKES ABOUT 2 CUPS

40 garlic cloves or 1 heaping cup garlic cloves, smashed
½ cup extra virgin olive oil
¼ cup light olive oil
2 tablespoons plus 2 teaspoons soy sauce (we use Kikkoman brand)
3 tablespoons whole grain mustard

Combine all ingredients except oils in non-reactive mixing bowl. Add oils gradually while whisking to incorporate.

BBQ RUB

½ cup chipotle in adobo, puréed
1 cup brown sugar
1 tablespoon Chili Mélange (see page 242)
1 teaspoon smoked paprika or good quality
1–2 teaspoons Spanish paprika
½ teaspoon garlic powder
1 teaspoon kosher salt
¼ freshly ground black pepper

Combine ingredients and store refrigerated in an airtight container.

TRADITIONAL MAYONNAISE

6 egg yolks
1 tablespoon plus 2 teaspoons mustard
2 teaspoons kosher salt
Pinch of white pepper
2 tablespoons freshly squeezed lemon juice
3 cups light oil

1 In non-reactive mixing bowl or food processor whisk or pulse together egg yolks, mustard, salt and pepper, and 1 tablespoon lemon juice.

2 Add oil in a slow steady stream while whisking to emulsify.

3 When about ¾ of the oil has been incorporated – add remaining tablespoon of lemon juice.

LEMON SCENTED MAYONNAISE

3 egg yolks
2 tablespoons water
4 teaspoons fresh lemon juice
2 teaspoons Tabasco
1 tablespoon sriracha (we use Shark brand)*
½ teaspoon kosher salt
1 cup light olive oil
½ cup extra virgin olive oil
½ cup finely sliced scallions
Zest of 1 lemon

1 Combine first 6 ingredients in food processor.

2 Drizzle in both oils in a slow, steady stream while food processor is running until thickened, but still light and supple.

3 Fold in scallions and lemon zest.

Available at most Asian markets.

SWEET CHILI MAYONNAISE

2 cups Traditional Mayonnaise (recipe above) or use prepared
⅓ cup sweet chili sauce, or more to taste (we use Mae Ploy brand)*

Stir together mayonnaise and sweet chili sauce in mixing bowl until desired flavor.

Available at most Asian Markets.

BALSAMIC REDUCTION

MAKES ABOUT 1 CUP

1½ cups balsamic vinegar
1 cup heavy whipping cream
½ cup whole garlic cloves
Kosher salt, to taste
Freshly ground black pepper, to taste

1   Reduce balsamic vinegar to a syrup by simmering very gently over low heat.

2   Add heavy whipping cream and garlic and simmer to reduce slightly – about 5 minutes.

3   Strain to remove garlic and season to taste with kosher salt and freshly ground black pepper.

BALSAMIC VINAIGRETTE

MAKES 1 ¾ CUPS

½ cup balsamic vinegar
2 tablespoons shallots, minced
1 tablespoon garlic
½ teaspoon kosher salt
¼ teaspoon freshly ground black pepper
½ cup extra virgin olive oil
½ cup light cooking oil
1 tablespoon fresh thyme leaves, chopped

1   Combine vinegar, shallots, garlic, and kosher salt and freshly ground black pepper in a non-reactive mixing bowl.

2   Add oil in a slow, steady stream while whisking to emulsify.

3   Add thyme and adjust seasoning.

GUAVA CITRUS VINAIGRETTE

MAKES ABOUT 2 ½ CUPS

⅓ cup lemon juice
⅓ cup fresh lime juice
⅓ cup fresh blood orange juice (or fresh orange juice if not available)
½ cup Guava Paste (see page 233) (or use Goya brand in round tins)*
¾ cup light olive oil
1 shallot, minced
¾ teaspoon (or to taste), hot smoked paprika
¾ teaspoon (or to taste), sweet smoked paprika
Kosher salt
Freshly ground black pepper, to taste

Combine everything, except olive oil in a food processor and purée – add oil in a slow steady stream while food processor is running to emulsify.

Available at most Latino and some Asian markets.

SESAME GINGER VINAIGRETTE

MAKES ABOUT 3 ½ CUPS

½ cup fresh ginger, minced
3 tablespoons garlic, minced
¼ cup unseasoned rice wine vinegar (we use Marukan brand)*
¼ cup hot sauce (we use Tiger Sauce brand)
¼ cup plus 1 tablespoon sweet chili sauce (we use Mae Ploy brand)*
Kosher salt
Freshly ground black pepper
¼ cup sesame oil
1¾ cups light olive oil

1   Combine all ingredients except oils in food processor and purée.

2   Add oil while food processor is running in slow steady stream to emulsify.

Available at most Asian markets.

SPICY THAI PEANUT VINAIGRETTE

MAKES ABOUT 3 ½ CUPS

¼ cup sesame oil
½ cup Thai sweet chili sauce (we use Mae Ploy brand)*
1 cup sherry (we use Lustau Amontillado Sherry)
¼ cup soy sauce (we use Kikkoman brand)*
½ cup peanut butter
¼ cup sriracha (we use Shark brand)*
¼ cup fresh ginger, minced
⅛ cup garlic, minced
2 tablespoons extra virgin olive oil
3 tablespoons unseasoned rice wine vinegar (we use Marukan brand)*
Kosher salt
Freshly ground black pepper

1 Combine everything except olive oil and rice wine vinegar in a non-reactive mixing bowl.

2 Transfer ingredients into a non-reactive saucepan and reduce over low heat until thickened – when thick, remove from heat and let cool slightly.

3 Add rice wine vinegar and then add extra virgin olive oil in a slow, steady stream while whisking to emulsify.

4 Add kosher salt and freshly ground black pepper if needed.

*Available at most Asian markets.

SWEET FIG VINAIGRETTE

MAKES ABOUT 2 ½ CUPS

2 teaspoons Dijon mustard
¾ cup sherry vinegar
½ cup Fig Preserves (see page 211) or Adriatic Fig Preserves*
Kosher salt
Freshly ground black pepper
¾ cup walnut oil

1 Combine all ingredients except walnut oil in a non-reactive mixing bowl.

2 Add walnut oil in a slow steady stream while whisking to emulsify.

*Available at Whole Foods Market, see sources, page 248.

SMOKEY TOMATO VINAIGRETTE

MAKES 2 ¾ CUPS

2 cups Smokey Tomato Salsa (see page 219)
3 tablespoons white wine vinegar
½ cup extra virgin olive oil

1 Stir together salsa and vinegar in a non-reactive mixing bowl.

2 Add extra virgin olive oil in a slow and steady stream while whisking to emulsify.

TRIPLE BLUE CHEESE DRESSING

MAKES ABOUT 4 CUPS

½ yellow onion, minced
1 shallot, minced
1½ cups mayonnaise
⅓ cup Maytag blue cheese, broken into
   large chunks
⅓ cup Rosenbourg blue cheese, broken into
   large chunks
⅓ cup Gorgonzola, broken into large chunks
3 tablespoons fresh sage, rough chop
1 tablespoon plus 1 teaspoon lemon juice
½ cup buttermilk
½ teaspoon kosher salt
¼ teaspoon freshly ground black pepper
Pinch of white pepper

Combine all in a non-reactive mixing bowl and adjust
seasonings to taste.

BASIL WALNUT PESTO

MAKES ABOUT 2 CUPS

1 quart basil leaves, firmly packed
1 cup walnuts
6 whole garlic cloves, or more to taste
¼ cup aged provolone, or more to taste
¼ cup Parmigiano Reggiano, or more to taste
½ cup extra virgin olive oil
Kosher salt
Freshly ground black pepper

1 Combine all ingredients except olive oil in food
   processor and pulse a few times to begin to
   combine ingredients.

2 Add olive oil in a slow, steady stream while food
   processor is running.

3 Adjust to taste.

CRÈME FRAÎCHE

MAKES 2 CUPS

1 cup sour cream
1 cup whipping cream

1 In a mixing bowl, stir together sour cream and
   whipping cream until smooth.

2 Cover and keep at warm room temperature for
   15 hours.

3 Refrigerate 24 hours before serving.

COCONUT MILK

MAKES ABOUT 1½ CUPS

1 cup firmly packed freshly grated coconut
1 cup boiling water

1 Combine coconut and boiling water and let rest
   for 30 minutes.

2 Place in food processor and purée.

3 Strain through doubled cheesecloth, pressing
   to extract as much flavor as possible.

PURÉE OF CURRIED ROAST PUMPKIN, SWEET POTATOES AND APPLES

MAKES ABOUT 5 QUARTS

There are a couple of sauces that are so good that we have served them as soup and a couple of soups that were so rich and delicious we've used them as sauces. This is one of those sauces – we have served it alongside roast pork, braised rabbit and any other excuse we could find to serve it. This is another example of not being locked into what something is "supposed" to be.

Extra virgin olive oil
Salted butter
1 large Spanish onion, fine julienne (about 2 cups)
Kosher salt
Freshly ground black pepper
1 large pie pumpkin, cut into wedges (about 2 pounds)
1–1½ teaspoons, or to taste hot curry powder* – good quality or mix yourself (see page 234)
2 large sweet potatoes, cut into large cubes
2 large Granny Smith apples, sliced
3 cups Chicken Essence (see page 68) stock or broth (If using canned broth, use College Inn brand.)
2 cups half and half
¾ cup Brown Sugar Spice (see page 242)
2 tablespoons Curry Spice Variation One (see page 238) or your favorite curry powder
1 tablespoon plus 1 teaspoon sriracha (we use Shark brand)**

1 Combine curry spices and set aside.

2 Preheat oven to 475°F.

3 Sauté onions in olive oil in large non-reactive saucepan until very soft – season with kosher salt and pepper.

4 Sprinkle pumpkin wedges generously with olive oil, kosher salt and pepper and roast in oven until soft and starting to brown and blister. Remove from oven and scoop flesh from skin.

5 Roast sweet potatoes as you did the pumpkin above.

6 Sauté apples with small amount of olive oil and butter in large sauté pan – season with 1 teaspoon of the Curry Spice.

7 Purée pumpkins, sweet potatoes, apples, and onions in batches in food processor.

8 Combine purées in large, non-reactive stock pot. Add chicken stock or broth, Brown Sugar Spice, sriracha, Curry Spice and kosher salt and freshly ground black pepper (to taste) and bring to a simmer.

9 Add half and half and continue to simmer until purée thickens slightly.

10 Adjust seasonings generously to taste.

Available through Penzeys Spices, see sources, page 248.
**Available at most Asian markets.*

GUAVA PASTE

MAKES ONE STANDARD LOAF PAN

2 pounds guavas, peeled
1½ cups water
4 cups sugar
1 tablespoon lime juice

1   Halve guavas and scoop out seeds – soak seeds
    in 1 cup water.

2   Place guavas in a non-reactive saucepan with
    remaining water, bring to a boil, reduce the heat
    to a simmer and cook the guavas until they are very
    soft being careful not to allow guavas to scorch.

3   Strain water with seeds and add that water to
    the guavas – discard the seeds.

4   Grind the guavas through the fine disk of a
    food grinder.

5   Measure the pulp and add an equal amount of
    sugar, mixing well. Place in a large, heavy saucepan
    over low heat and cook, stirring constantly with
    a wooden spoon, until the mixture becomes thick.
    Remove from heat and transfer to an electric mixing
    bowl. Beat with a paddle until the mixture forms
    a heavy paste – about 10 minutes.

6   Store in airtight container or create mold by lining
    loaf pan with wax paper and filling with Guava Paste
    – refrigerate 8 hours to set and then turn out and
    wrap with film wrap and then aluminum foil.

PASSION FRUIT BEURRE BLANC

MAKES ABOUT 1½ CUPS

2 shallots, minced
1 cup good quality, dry white wine
½ pound or 2 sticks salted butter, cold and cut into
   tablespoons
3 tablespoons Crème Fraîche (see page 231)
1 tablespoon fresh passion fruit, puréed or
   condensed passion fruit drink*
Pinch of brown sugar
Pinch of kosher salt
Pinch of freshly ground black pepper

1   Place minced shallots, salt and pepper and white
    wine in a non-reactive pan and reduce at a gentle
    simmer to reduce until liquid is almost completely
    gone.

2   Over very low heat, add butter, one tablespoon at a
    time, while whisking, until butter is incorporated and
    sauce has thickened. You may have to pull pan on
    and off of heat during the process to prevent sauce
    from breaking. Whisk in Crème Fraîche, brown sugar
    and passion fruit purée – taste and adjust seasonings.
    Remove from heat, cover and keep in a warm place
    until ready to use.

Available at most Asian markets.

SPICE MIXTURES
AND AROMATIC OILS

MISO LEMON GRASS OIL

This is a large batch because we use it to prepare the Confit of New England Swordfish – feel free to cut in half to keep on hand for a myriad of other uses.

8 cups canola/peanut oil
2 cups light olive oil
1½ cups whole garlic cloves
2 cups lemon grass, slices
¼ cup Szechuan peppercorns*
1 package miso paste, at room temperature
  (we use Shirakiku brand)*

1   Place oil and garlic cloves in heavy non-reactive pot and poach garlic for 30 minutes or until garlic is soft and oil is fragrant. Raise heat to high and oil is just below a simmer.

2   Reduce heat to medium and add lemon grass and peppercorns. Ingredients should sizzle, puff up and become aromatic. Remove from heat and allow to sit for 10 minutes.

3   Temper miso by adding some oil to it to soften and then adding miso back into oil.

4   Allow oil to cool to room temperature and then strain through a china cap or fine mesh sieve, pressing with the back side of a ladle to extract as much flavor as possible from aromatics.

5   Store refrigerated in an airtight container.

*Available at most Asian markets.

CHILI OIL

This is a delicious and versatile Asian style chili oil.

3 cups peanut oil
1 cup favorite dried red chilies, rough chop or
  ½ cup flakes
½ cup crushed red chili
5 garlic cloves, peeled and smashed
2 tablespoons fresh ginger, minced
½ cup fermented black beans or black bean paste*
¾ cup sesame oil

1   Pulse and then purée all ingredients except sesame oil together in food processor.

2   Combine all ingredients in a medium, non-reactive saucepan over medium heat until just below simmer. Ingredients should sizzle, puff up and become aromatic.

3   Turn heat to low and continue cooking for about 5 minutes.

4   Remove from the stove and allow to cool to room temperature. Strain through fine chinois or double layer of cheesecloth adding sesame oil as you pour through chinois to incorporate. Press ingredients with the back of a ladle to extract as much flavor as possible.

5   Store refrigerated in an airtight container.

*Available at most Asian markets.

ANNATTO OIL

MAKES ABOUT 2 CUPS

Annatto has a subtle, nutty flavor and adds beautiful golden color to a dish. It is traditionally used in Latin American, Caribbean, Puerto Rican and Filipino cooking – You can use it in many applications, from including it when preparing rice and grains to just drizzling it on a plate as a beautiful adornment.

2 cups light olive oil
1 cup annatto seeds (also called achiote)

1   Combine olive oil and annatto seeds in small, non-reactive saucepan over medium heat and cook gently for about 5 minutes stirring occasionally. Remove from the stove.

2 Allow to cool to room temperature.

3 Strain and store refrigerated in an airtight container.

Available at most Latino markets and through Penzey's Spices, see sources, page 248.

CURRY LEAF OIL

MAKES ABOUT 2 CUPS

Curry leaves have an amazing smell and give amazing flavor – toasty, nutty and reminiscent of curry spices.

2 cups light cooking oil
3 stalks fresh curry leaves*, lightly crushed

1   Combine olive oil and 2 stalks curry leaves in small non-reactive saucepan over medium heat for about 5 minutes stirring occasionally.

2   Remove from stove and allow to cool to room temperature.

3   Strain.

4   Add remaining stalk of curry leaves.

5   Store refrigerated in an airtight container.

*Available at many Asian and Middle Eastern grocers.

CURRY SPICE VARIATION ONE

MAKES ABOUT 1 CUP

This is a short-cut, but delicious curry spice blend.

½ cup sweet curry powder*
½ cup hot curry powder*
¼ cup kosher salt
3 tablespoons ground coriander
1 tablespoon ground turmeric
1 teaspoon cayenne

Combine well and store in an airtight container in a cool, dry place.

*Available through Penzeys, see sources, page 248.

CURRY SPICE VARIATION TWO

Make this blend for the freshest and most authentic method of preparing a curry spice blend – experiment with different spices and proportions to suit your palate.
.

1½ cups coriander seeds
¼ cup cumin seeds
1½ teaspoons ground ginger
1½ teaspoons cumin seeds
1½ teaspoons mustard seeds
1½ teaspoons fenugreek
1 teaspoon ground turmeric
½ teaspoon whole cloves
1 cinnamon stick
2 cardamom seeds
4 black peppercorns
1 dried red chile, seeded
2 pinches saffron

1 Preheat oven to 250ºF.

2 Place all ingredients except saffron on sheet tray and roast about 15 minutes until aromatic shaking pan several times as spices roast.

3 Grind in batches in spice mill or coffee grinder with saffron until smooth.

4 Combine well and store in an airtight container in a cool, dry place.

GARAM MASALA

MAKES ABOUT ¾ CUP

This spice blend has a high proportion of the lemony, flowery scented cardamom and along with the cloves and cinnamon it has a highly aromatic nose, almost giving the impression of sweetness.

2½–3-inch pieces of cinnamon stick
½ cup whole green cardamom pods
¼ cup cloves
¼ cup whole cumin
2 tablespoons whole coriander
¼ cup whole black peppercorn

1 Preheat the oven to 250°F.

2 Spread the spices out in one layer on a baking sheet; toast on the bottom shelf of the oven until aromatic – about 30 minutes, stirring and turning the mixture several times. Do not let the spices burn or turn brown.

3 Sort the spices. Crack the cinnamon into shards using a mallet or rolling pin.

4 Mix all of the spices in a bowl then grind in small batches in a spice mill or coffee grinder until smooth.

5 Combine well and store in an airtight container in a cool, dry place.

MOROCCAN SPICE

MAKES ABOUT 1 CUP

1 tablespoon plus ½ teaspoon ground cumin
1 tablespoon plus ½ teaspoon ground ginger
2 tablespoons ground coriander
2 teaspoons plus 1 teaspoon freshly ground pepper
2½ teaspoons cayenne
2 teaspoons urfat isot (Turkish pepper)*
2½ teaspoons ground cloves
⅓ cup allspice
1 tablespoon plus 2 teaspoons cinnamon
1 tablespoon plus 2 teaspoons kosher salt

Combine well and store in an airtight container in a cool, dry place.

Available through Savory Spice Shop, see sources, page 248.

CHILI MÉLANGE

MAKES ABOUT 1 CUP

If you can't find some of the chiles included in the recipe – don't worry about it – it will still be delicious.

2 tablespoons ground chili powder
2 tablespoons ground paprika
2 tablespoons ground coriander
1 tablespoon garlic powder
1 tablespoon plus 1 teaspoon ground cumin
3 teaspoons ground cayenne
2 teaspoons crushed red pepper
3 teaspoons dried oregano
2 tablespoons kosher salt
2 teaspoons freshly ground black pepper
½ teaspoon ground ancho chile
¼ teaspoon urfat isot (Turkish pepper)*
¼ teaspoon ground habanero chile

Combine well and store in an airtight container in a cool, dry place.

*Available through Savory Spice Shop, see sources, page 248.

BROWN SUGAR SPICE

MAKES ABOUT 1 ¾ CUPS

1½ cups brown sugar
1½ teaspoons cinnamon
½ teaspoon allspice
¼ teaspoon cloves
¼ teaspoon nutmeg
¼ cup crystallized ginger, finely minced
¾ teaspoon kosher salt

Combine well and store in an airtight container in a cool, dry place.

FAJITA SPICE

MAKES ABOUT 2 CUPS

1 cup paprika
¼ cup plus 1 tablespoon cayenne
½ cup kosher salt
2 tablespoons freshly ground black pepper or to taste

Combine well and store in an airtight container in a cool, dry place.

ABRAHAM'S TENT IS OPEN ON ALL FOUR SIDES

Once, while conducting an interview, I was trying to convey my philosophy about hospitality in the restaurant. Suddenly, I looked at the person I was interviewing and said, "you're Jewish aren't you? Well, you know how in the Torah it says Abraham's tent was open on all four sides…well, that is what I want for the restaurant – anybody who comes here should feel welcomed and taken care of." Meanwhile, our manager at the time, who was sitting next to me conducting the interview was kicking me under the table, scribbling on her notepad – you can't ask if someone is Jewish Eve! I guess that wasn't the most suitable interview question – but I was just trying to get my point across and that was the image I had from my own upbringing. The person who I was interviewing ended up taking the position, doing a great job and becoming a great friend to the restaurant – and the idea I had for the restaurant as almost a sanctuary for people – where they would always be welcome and taken care of is still the foundation of our philosophy.

MOROCCAN SEASONED FLOUR

MAKES ABOUT 2 ¼ CUPS

1 cup Moroccan Spice (see page 239)
1 cup flour
6 teaspoons kosher salt
½ teaspoon urfat isot (Turkish pepper)*

Combine well and store in an airtight container in a cool dark place.

Available through Savory Spice Shop, see sources, page 248.

CURRY SPICE SEASONED FLOUR

MAKES ABOUT 3 ½ CUPS

2 cups flour
1½ cups Curry Spice (see pages 234)
3 tablespoons kosher salt

Combine well and store in an airtight container in a cool, dry place.

CHILI MÉLANGE SEASONED FLOUR

MAKES ABOUT 2 ½ CUPS

2 cups all-purpose flour
⅓ cup Chili Mélange (see page 242)
2 teaspoons kosher salt

Combine well and store in an airtight container.

SPICED CORNMEAL

MAKES ABOUT 5 ½ CUPS

We use both yellow and white cornmeal, but feel free to use whichever you have on hand.

2 cups white cornmeal
2 cups yellow cornmeal
1 cup Chili Mélange (see page 242)
½ cup kosher salt

Combine well and store in an airtight container.

MISO BROWN SUGAR RUB

MAKES ABOUT 2 CUPS

1 cup Aromatic Paste (reserved from
 Miso Lemon Grass Oil, page 236)
1¼ cup Brown Sugar Spice (see page 242)

Combine well and store refrigerated in an airtight
container.

LAVENDER AND WILDFLOWER HONEY RUB

MAKES ABOUT 1½ CUPS

2 tablespoons anchovy paste (puréed anchovy fillets)
24 cloves crushed garlic
½ cup extra virgin olive oil
1½ teaspoons brown sugar
1 teaspoon wild flower honey*
3 tablespoons herbs de Provence
3 tablespoons whole grain mustard

Combine all ingredients in food processor.

*Available at Cohoctah Honey Works, see sources,
page 248.*

SEASONAL AVAILABILITY CHART

Through the year, we wait for our favorite ingredients to come into season and often the period that they are available feels way too short – This is a quick guide that will help you watch out for your favorites so you don't miss catching them while they are at their prime

JANUARY
Blood Oranges
Grapefruit
Kumquats
Oranges
Sweet Potatoes
Black Truffles
Black Trumpet Mushrooms
Hedgehog Mushrooms
Matsutake Mushrooms
Duck
Monkfish
Oysters
Sea urchins

FEBRUARY
Blood oranges
Grapefruit
Kumquats
Passion Fruit
Black Truffles
Black Trumpet Mushrooms
Hedgehog Mushrooms
Monkfish
Oysters

MARCH
Lychees
Passion Fruit
Rhubarb
Artichokes
New Potatoes
Snow Peas
Sugar Snap Peas
Oysters
Stone Crabs

APRIL
Rhubarb
Artichokes
Asparagus
New Potatoes
Ramps
Snow Peas
Sugar Snap Peas
Turnips
Morels
Goose Eggs
Oysters
Shad Roe
Smelt
Stone Crabs

MAY
Lychees
Mangos
Rhubarb
Asparagus
Fiddleheads
Turnips
Vidalia Onions
Cepes
Chanterelles
Morels
Bluefish
Conch
Dungeness Crabs
Sardines
Soft Shell Crabs
Shad Roe

JUNE
Apricots
Cherries
Figs
Lychees
Mangos
Strawberries
Fiddleheads
Okra
Squash Blossoms
Summer Squash
Vidalia Onions
Cepes
Chanterelles
Morels
Bluefish
Clams
Conch
Crayfish
Dungeness Crabs
King Salmon
Naragansatt Squid
Soft Shell Crabs
Spanish Sardines
Tuna

JULY
Apricots
Cherries
Currants
Figs
Gooseberries
Mangos
Peaches
Watermelon
Corn
Eggplant
English Peas
Okra
Seabeans
Squash Blossoms
Summer Squash
Tomatoes
Chanterelles
White Truffles
Clams
Dungeness Crabs
King Salmon
Massachusettes Swordfish
Soft Shell Crabs
Spanish Sardines
Tuna

AUGUST	SEPTEMBER	OCTOBER	NOVEMBER	DECEMBER
Apricots	Apples	Apples	Cranberries	Blood Oranges
Blueberries	Asian Pears	Asian Pears	Dates	Cranberries
Figs	Cranberries	Cranberries	Kumquats	Dates
Gooseberries	Gooseberries	Dates	Pomegranates	Kumquats
Mangos	Plums	Figs	Pumpkin	Pumpkins
Peaches	Pomegranates	Kumquats	Sweet Potatoes	Sweet Potatoes
Plums	Pumpkins	Pears	Black Trumpet Mushrooms	Black Truffles
Watermelon	Corn	Pomegranates	Cepes	Black Trumpet mushrooms
Corn	Eggplant	Pumpkin	Matsutake Mushrooms	Hedgehog Mushrooms
Eggplant	Black Trumpet Mushrooms	Seabeans	Chanterelles	Lobster Mushrooms
Okra	Cepes	Black Trumpet Mushrooms	Hedgehogs	Matsutake Mushrooms
Seabeans	Chanterelles	Cepes	Lobster Mushrooms	Duck
Squash Blossoms	Lobster Mushrooms	Chanterelles	Abalone	Monkfish
Summer Squash	Matsutake Mushrooms	Lobster Mushrooms	Duck	Nantucket Bay Scallops
Tomatoes	King Salmon	Hedgehog Mushrooms	Nantucket Bay Scallops	Oysters
Chanterelles	Maine Lobster	Matsutake Mushrooms	Oysters	Pigeon
Lobster Mushrooms	New England Swordfish	Abalone	Pigeon	
White Truffles	Oysters	Bluefish	Rabbit	
Clams	Squab	Duck	Stone Crabs	
Dungeness Crabs	Tuna	King Salmon		
King Salmon		Nantucket Bay Scallops		
Maine Lobster		New England Swordfish		
Naragansatt Squid		Oysters		
New England Swordfish		Rabbit		
Squab				
Tuna				

Ann Arbor Farmer's Market
315 Detroit Street
Ann Arbor, MI 48104
734.944.3276

Wide variety of seasonal and locally grown fruits and vegetables and herbs

From our recipes: seasonal berries, lettuces, herbs, tomatoes, squash blossoms and other produce throughout the growing season

Asian Markets
Shark brand sriracha, Mae Ploy brand sweet chili sauce, Marukan unseasoned rice wine vinegar, Goya guava paste, Gari (pickled ginger), Ikura (Salmon roe), wakame, pea shoots, quails eggs, Kikkoman soy sauce, Kadoya brand sesame oil, Koon Shun brand hoisin and barbecue sauces, pickled plums, pomegranate molasses, kelp noodles, yam noodles and many more of my favorite ingredients

Avalon International Breads
422 West Willis
Detroit, MI 48201
313.832.0008

Organic, artisanally-made bread, pastries and other baked goods

Savory Spice Shop
savoryspiceshop.com

Turkish spices and foodstuffs

From our recipes: Urfat Isot

Cohoctah Honey Works
Ann Arbor Farmer's Market
or
7215 Geer Road
Howell, MI 48843
517-545-2447

All kinds of seasonal wild flower honey

From our recipes: Lavender and Wild Flower Honey Rub

D'artagnan Inc.
280 Wilson Avenue
Newark, NJ 07105
800.327.8246
www.dartagnan.com

Duck, lamb, foie gras, sausage

From our recipes: Lamb Fajitas, Sweet and Spicy Moulard Duck Breast, Sirloin of Lamb

Durham's Tracklements
212 East Kingsley
Ann Arbor, MI 48104
800.844.7853
www.tracklements.com

Duck fat, smoked and cured meats and fish

From our recipes: Haricots Verts, Fingerling Potatoes, Asian Smoked Salmon Tartare, 'Brandade in a Box', Stir Fried Cured Duck Salad, Smoked Cod Ceviche, Perfumed Pork Sausage

Heritage Foods USA
P.O. Box 827
New York, NY 10150
212.980.6603
www.heritagefoodsusa.com

Special breeds and varieties of pork, duck, lamb, beef, salmon, beans, cornmeal and other foodstuffs raised, grown and created with care around the country by family farmers and artisanal producers

From our recipes: Berkshire pork, Wagyu Beef

Monahan's Seafood Market
407 N. Fifth Avenue
Ann Arbor, MI 48104
734.662.5118

Super fresh fish and shellfish specializing in wild, seasonal and hard to find fish and shellfish, personal service and special requests

From our recipes: Whole Spanish octopus, Loup de Mer, Ikura salmon roe, soft shell crabs, quail eggs

Morgan and York
1928 Packard Road
Ann Arbor, MI 48104
734.662.0798
www.morganandyork.com

Artisanal cheeses, special and hard to find foodstuffs, wines and spirits

From our recipes: All kinds of Cheese, Pear Mostarda, Speck, Pommeau Du Normande

Niman Ranch
San Francisco, CA
866.808.0340
www.nimanranch.com

A network of family farms — Humanely and sustainably raised beef, lamb and pork

Penzeys Spice
17712 West 13 Mile Road
Beverly Hills, MI
248.647.6177
800.741.7787
www.penzeys.com

All kinds of freshly ground and mixed spices

From our recipes: too many to mention here

Roos Roast
410 West Huron Street
Ann Arbor, MI 48103
734.709.9565
www.roosroast.com

Freshly roasted coffee

Sparrow Meat Market
407 N. Fifth Avenue
Ann Arbor, MI 48104
734.761.8175
www.sparrowmeat.getwebnet.com

Fresh and cured meats, specializing in locally raised meat and poultry — beef, lamb, chicken, duck and rabbit

From our recipes: Ohio Bacon, speck, Michigan Rabbits, Cuban Reuben

Whole Foods
www.wholefoods.com

Seasonal and organic produce, sea beans, Adriatic Fig Preserves

Zingerman's Deli
422 Detroit Street
Ann Arbor, MI 48104
734.663.3354
www.zingermans.com

Artisanal cheeses, bread, sausage, olives, oils, vinegars, chocolate and other specialty foodstuffs

From our recipes: olives, bread, sausage, chocolate

ZZ's Market
4092 Packard Road
Ann Arbor, MI 48108
734.822.0494

Ethnic groceries of all kinds. Exotic produce, grains, cheese, spices

From our recipes: Shark brand Sriracha, Mae Ploy brand sweet chili sauce, El Ebro brand canned black beans, San Marcos brand canned Chipotles, Chaokoh coconut milk, Goya guava paste, fresh curry leaves, chilies, all kinds of exotic produce throughout the year